TONI
MORRISON

COMPREHENSIVE RESEARCH
AND STUDY GUIDE

BLOOM'S
MAJOR
NOVELISTS

EDITED AND WITH AN INTRODUCTION
BY HAROLD BLOOM

© 2000 by Chelsea House Publishers, a subsidiary of Haights Cross Communications.

Introduction © 2000 by Harold Bloom

Printed and bound in the United States of America.

3 5 7 9 8 6 4 2

Library of Congress Cataloging-in-Publication Data
Toni Morrison / edited and with an introduction by Harold Bloom.
    p.   cm. — (Bloom's major novelists)
Includes bibliographical references (p.   ) and index.
ISBN 0-7910-5258-3
1. Morrison, Toni—Examinations—Study guides.   2. Women and literature—United States—History—20th century.   3. Afro-Americans in literature.   I. Bloom, Harold.   II. Series.
PS3563.08749Z894   1999
813'.54—dc21   99-34234
                                                CIP

Chelsea House Publishers
1974 Sproul Road, Suite 400
Broomall, PA 19008-0914

The Chelsea House world wide web
address is www.chelseahouse.com

Contributing Editor: Tenley Williams

TONI
MORRISON

**COMPREHENSIVE RESEARCH
AND STUDY GUIDE**

BLOOM'S

MAJOR

NOVELISTS

**EDITED AND WITH AN
INTRODUCTION BY HAROLD BLOOM**

BLOOM'S MAJOR DRAMATISTS

Anton Chekhov
Henrik Ibsen
Arthur Miller
Eugene O'Neill
Shakespeare's Comedies
Shakespeare's Histories
Shakespeare's Romances
Shakespeare's Tragedies
George Bernard Shaw
Tennessee Williams

BLOOM'S MAJOR NOVELISTS

Jane Austen
The Brontës
Willa Cather
Charles Dickens
William Faulkner
F. Scott Fitzgerald
Nathaniel Hawthorne
Ernest Hemingway
Toni Morrison
John Steinbeck
Mark Twain
Alice Walker

BLOOM'S MAJOR SHORT STORY WRITERS

William Faulkner
F. Scott Fitzgerald
Ernest Hemingway
O. Henry
James Joyce
Herman Melville
Flannery O'Connor
Edgar Allan Poe
J. D. Salinger
John Steinbeck
Mark Twain
Eudora Welty

BLOOM'S MAJOR WORLD POETS

Geoffrey Chaucer
Emily Dickinson
John Donne
T. S. Eliot
Robert Frost
Langston Hughes
John Milton
Edgar Allan Poe
Shakespeare's Poems & Sonnets
Alfred, Lord Tennyson
Walt Whitman
William Wordsworth

BLOOM'S NOTES

The Adventures of Huckleberry Finn
Aeneid
The Age of Innocence
Animal Farm
The Autobiography of Malcolm X
The Awakening
Beloved
Beowulf
Billy Budd, Benito Cereno, & Bartleby the Scrivener
Brave New World
The Catcher in the Rye
Crime and Punishment
The Crucible

Death of a Salesman
A Farewell to Arms
Frankenstein
The Grapes of Wrath
Great Expectations
The Great Gatsby
Gulliver's Travels
Hamlet
Heart of Darkness & The Secret Sharer
Henry IV, Part One
I Know Why the Caged Bird Sings
Iliad
Inferno
Invisible Man
Jane Eyre
Julius Caesar

King Lear
Lord of the Flies
Macbeth
A Midsummer Night's Dream
Moby-Dick
Native Son
Nineteen Eighty-Four
Odyssey
Oedipus Plays
Of Mice and Men
The Old Man and the Sea
Othello
Paradise Lost
A Portrait of the Artist as a Young Man
The Portrait of a Lady

Pride and Prejudice
The Red Badge of Courage
Romeo and Juliet
The Scarlet Letter
Silas Marner
The Sound and the Fury
The Sun Also Rises
A Tale of Two Cities
Tess of the D'Urbervilles
Their Eyes Were Watching God
To Kill a Mockingbird
Uncle Tom's Cabin
Wuthering Heights

Contents

User's Guide

This volume is designed to present biographical, critical, and bibliographical information on the author's best-known or most important works. Following Harold Bloom's editor's note and introduction is a detailed biography of the author, discussing major life events and important literary accomplishments. A plot summary of each novel follows, tracing significant themes, patterns, and motifs in the work.

A selection of critical extracts, derived from previously published material from leading critics, analyzes aspects of each work. The extracts consist of statements from the author, if available, early reviews of the work, and later evaluations up to the present. A bibliography of the author's writings (including a complete list of all works written, cowritten, edited, and translated), a list of additional books and articles on the author and his or her work, and an index of themes and ideas in the author's writings conclude the volume.

Harold Bloom is Sterling Professor of the Humanities at Yale University and Henry W. and Albert A. Berg Professor of English at the New York University Graduate School. He is the author of over 20 books and the editor of more than 30 anthologies of literary criticism.

Professor Bloom's works include *Shelley's Mythmaking* (1959), *The Visionary Company* (1961), *Blake's Apocalypse* (1963), *Yeats* (1970), *A Map of Misreading* (1975), *Kabbalah and Criticism* (1975), and *Agon: Toward a Theory of Revisionism* (1982). *The Anxiety of Influence* (1973) sets forth Professor Bloom's provocative theory of the literary relationships between the great writers and their predecessors. His most recent books include *The American Religion* (1992), *The Western Canon* (1994), *Omens of Millennium: The Gnosis of Angels, Dreams, and Resurrection* (1996), and *Shakespeare: The Invention of the Human* (1998), a finalist for the 1998 National Book Award.

Professor Bloom earned his Ph.D. from Yale University in 1955 and has served on the Yale faculty since then. He is a 1985 MacArthur Foundation Award recipient, served as the Charles Eliot Norton Professor of Poetry at Harvard University in 1987–88, and has received honorary degrees from the universities of Rome and Bologna. In 1999, Professor Bloom received the prestigious American Academy of Arts and Letters Gold Medal for Criticism.

Currently, Harold Bloom is the editor of numerous Chelsea House volumes of literary criticism, including the series BLOOM'S NOTES, BLOOM'S MAJOR SHORT STORY WRITERS, BLOOM'S MAJOR POETS, MAJOR LITERARY CHARACTERS, MODERN CRITICAL VIEWS, MODERN CRITICAL INTERPRETATIONS, and WOMEN WRITERS OF ENGLISH AND THEIR WORKS.

Editor's Note

My Introduction is a brief appreciation of *Song of Solomon*, much Toni Morrison's best work, in my judgment.

The Critical Views reflect the almost exclusively political emphasis of criticism devoted to Morrison. In this, her exegetes follow Morrison's own insistence that she is to be interpreted as an African-American nationalist and as a Marxist feminist. Her admirers also honor her assertion that her work is to be studied in the context of African-American literature, despite her palpable affiliations with William Faulkner and Virginia Woolf.

Introduction

HAROLD BLOOM

Song of Solomon remains Morrison's strongest novel, if only because its powers of invention do not yield their primacy to Morrison's ideological concerns. Milkman Dead is Morrison's most complex and equivocal protagonist, and therefore her most interesting.

Milkman Dead is a quester, in search of his true identity, and owes something crucial to Faulkner's Joe Christmas, of *Light in August*. Journeying to Shalimar, Virginia, in search of his family past, Milkman is told the story of "the flying African," his ancestor, Solomon or Shalimar, who is reputed to have flown back to Africa.

Rather subtly, Morrison stages a visionary argument between Milkman Dead and the nameless protagonist of Ralph Ellison's *Invisible Man*. Ellison's Invisible Man is a much richer personality than Morrison's Milkman; of these two involuntary disciples of Faulkner, Ellison remains the greater artist, despite Morrison's fecundity. Nevertheless, Morrison is impressive when she contrasts Milkman's death-leap, his Song of Solomon, with Invisible Man's underground existence, in a juxtaposition of the two novels' final stances:

> Step outside the narrow borders of what men call reality and you step into chaos . . . or imagination. That too I've learned in the cellar, and not by deadening my sense of perception; I'm invisible, not blind.

> As fleet and light as a lodestar he wheeled toward Guitar and it did not matter which one of them would give up his ghost in the killing arms of his brother. For now he knew what Shalimar knew: If you surrendered to the air, you could *ride* it.

Milkman Dead's flight is a "step into chaos," from Invisible Man's perspective. But the underground liberation of Ellison's wise protagonist is answered by the great unwisdom of Milkman's death-leap: an heroic attempt to *ride* chaos. ❀

Biography of Toni Morrison

Toni Morrison was born Chloe Anthony Wofford on February 18, 1931, in the northern Ohio city of Lorain, the second of four children of George and Ramah Willis Wofford. Grandfather Willis had moved his family from Kentucky to Ohio in search of a better life; her father, a Georgia sharecropper, came north to work as a shipyard welder. Among the legacies from her family that influenced Morrison's life and writing are a strong, black self-image; examples of maternal authority and equality in marriage; and the power of black community. George Wofford imparted to his daughter a strong sense of black identity. Ramah Wofford, counseling her daughter against crippling hatred, became a model for the powerful and resourceful women in Morrison's fiction. From her maternal grandparents, John Solomon and Ardelia Willis, Morrison heard stories of the post-Reconstruction South; from the black community's oral tradition Morrison heard terrifying and inspiring stories about black history and the Underground Railroad. About her roots as a writer, Morrison would later remark, "[T]he range of emotions and perceptions I have had access to as a black person and a female person are greater than those of people who are neither. . . . My world did not shrink because I was a black female writer. It just got bigger."

From early childhood Morrison was an accomplished storyteller and reader, expected to excel in school. She read widely in the works of English, French, and Russian novelists, and about the writings and accomplishments of African Americans. In 1949 Morrison graduated from Lorain High School and entered Howard University, where she changed her name to Toni. As a member of the Howard Unity Players, the university repertory company, she toured the South. Graduating with a B.A. in English in 1953, Morrison enrolled at Cornell University, receiving an M.A. in English in 1955 for her thesis on the theme of suicide in the novels of William Faulkner and Virginia Woolf. She taught English at Texas Southern University (1955–57) and at Howard University (1957–64). During her years at Howard she married Jamaican architect Harold Morrison, with whom she had two sons, Harold Ford Morrison, born in 1962, and Slade Kevin Morrison, born in 1965.

Divorced from her husband in 1964, Toni Morrison returned to Lorain with her children. By 1965 she had become an editor for a textbook subsidiary of Random House in Syracuse, New York. In 1967, she accepted a position at Random House in New York City and became a senior editor in 1968, a position she held until 1985. As senior editor, Morrison nurtured the talents of black writers such as Angela Davis and Toni Cade Bambara. Her own first novel, *The Bluest Eye*, set in the African-American community in Lorain, Ohio, was published in 1970.

Morrison was Associate Professor of English at the State University of New York at Purchase in 1969, when she began work on her second novel. *Sula*, and an edition of Middleton Harris's *The Black Book*, were published in 1973. *Sula* was nominated for the 1975 National Book Award, received the Ohioana Book Award, and was featured as a Book-of-the-Month Club Alternate. While Morrison was a visiting Lecturer at Yale University (1975–77), her third novel, *Song of Solomon*, was published; it received the National Book Critics Circle Award and the American Academy and Institute of Arts and Letters Award in 1977. *Tar Baby* was published in 1981. While a Schweitzer Professor of the Humanities at the State University of New York at Albany (1984–89), Morrison received the New York State Governor's Art Award (1986) and was a visiting lecturer at Bard College (1986–88). Her next novel, *Beloved*, was nominated for the 1987 National Book Award and the National Book Critics Award, and was awarded both the 1988 Pulitzer Prize for fiction and the Robert F. Kennedy Award. Morrison has suggested that *Beloved* and her 1992 novel, *Jazz*, constitute the first and second books in a planned trilogy. Her most recent novel, *Paradise*, was published in 1998.

In addition to literature, Morrison has written lyrics for Jessye Norman and collaborated with André Previn to write lyrics for songs sung by Kathleen Battle. She is a trustee of the National Humanities Center, co-chair of the Schomburg Commission for the Preservation of Black Culture, and a member of the American Academy and Institute of Arts and Letters, the American Academy of Arts and Sciences, the National Council on the Arts, the Authors Guild, and the Authors League of America. She has received the Elizabeth Cady Stanton Award from the National Organization for Women and the 1993 Nobel Prize for Literature, as well as honorary degrees from Oberlin College, Dartmouth College, Bryn Mawr College, and Columbia and Yale Universities.

Since 1989 Morrison has been Robert F. Goheen Professor of the Humanities at Princeton University. ❀

Plot Summary of
The Bluest Eye

Here is the house. The first paragraph of *The Bluest Eye* seems identical to a once commonly used, first-grade reading book depicting a white, middle-class American family. In the appearance of the daughter, blue-eyed and blonde-haired, Pecola Breedlove, a lonely, eleven-year-old black girl sees the ideal of American beauty that, if she could only achieve it, would ensure that she, too, would be loved. In the second paragraph, the same excerpt is repeated, but without punctuation. The paragraph is repeated once more, but without any sensible form, as a sign of Pecola's madness. These fragments from the primer, repeated throughout the novel, emphasize the gulf between black and white cultures, between white standards of beauty and the impossible imposition of them upon a black aesthetic.

Quiet as it's kept, there were no marigolds in the fall of 1941. Claudia MacTeer begins a retrospective narration about Pecola and events that occurred during the fall of 1941. She seems to take us into her confidence to relate what had once been only whispered about. An omniscient narrator will weave into Claudia's narration other information that will shape our understanding of Pecola's life. Here, Claudia tells us that no marigolds had bloomed that fall because, the children thought, Pecola was having her father's baby. Claudia tells us that Cholly had seeded "his own plot of black dirt." But this "black dirt," usually ascribed to the richest soil, yields no life. Cholly's self-hatred is ironically reflected in his name, Breedlove. He is unable to love; only to perform the act of breeding, in this case, with his daughter. The stillborn child is a sign of the self-hatred that breeds only more of the same.

Nuns go by as quiet as lust . . . In Autumn 1940, Claudia and her older sister, Frieda, have just started school. Claudia is nine years old, in bed with a cold, lovingly attended by her mother. Pecola is placed, for a few days, by a county agency in the MacTeer household, her father having burned down his family's home. Claudia recalls that Pecola unexpectedly begins menstruating. Frieda tells Pecola that now she is ready to find someone to love her. Pecola is overwhelmed by this news: To her knowledge, no one has ever loved her.

To Mrs. MacTeer's annoyance, Pecola drinks all the milk in the house. Pecola is fascinated by the Shirley Temple drinking mug, and seems intent on devouring this golden-haired symbol of white charm with the milk. Claudia, in contrast, is less charmed by whiteness: She is unimpressed by the mug and, when she is at last deemed worthy to be given a pink-faced, yellow-haired doll, she dismembers it.

HEREISTHEHOUSE . . . HEREISTHEFAMILY. The omniscient narrator describes other memories of Pecola's family: Pecola and her brother listen to the violent quarreling of their mother and their drunken father. Amidst terrible poverty and violence, Pecola prays for blue eyes, believing that, if she were so beautiful, the world would reflect it; everything would be better. From the day she is born, Pecola is called "ugly," her mother more concerned with her child's distance from white ideals of "appearance" than in the child's health. Pecola learns early to hate herself because of her blackness.

In **Winter**, Claudia remembers "the disrupter," Maureen Peal, a light-skinned black girl whose appearance is always clean and thought to be perfect, with her long, straight hair (her two long braids are described as "lynch ropes"), green eyes, and pretty clothes. A protruding, fang-like tooth does not detract from the fact that she has light, "high yellow," skin. She is popular, unlike Pecola, who is generally despised because she is poor, very black, and considered ugly. During a quarrel between Maureen and the sisters, Claudia, intending to slug Maureen, hits Pecola instead. Maureen flees, turning only to shout back at them, "I *am* cute! And you ugly!" Pecola is hurt and miserable.

In **Spring**, Claudia recalls how she and Frieda were introduced to the peculiarities of adult sexuality when their border, Mr. Henry, touches Frieda's breasts. Mr. MacTeer tries to kill him, insisting that Frieda could be "ruined." Claudia and her sister think the term means "fat," and they seek out Pecola, whose father is a drunk, in their belief that liquor will "eat up" fat. A comical moment becomes something else when Pauline cruelly upbraids her daughter for dropping a pan of cobbler, although Pecola has badly burned herself. By contrast, Pauline is solicitous to the daughter of her employer, who calls her "Polly." Pecola calls her mother "Mrs. Breedlove."

The omniscient narrator intrudes to tell us about the early life of Pecola's mother (**SEETHEMOTHER**), Pauline Breedlove; her marriage to Cholly and the births of Pecola and Sammy. After Pauline's story, we learn about Cholly's terrible childhood and adolescence, to the time of his marriage to Pauline Williams (**SEETHEFATHER**). One day, Cholly stumbles home, drunk, and rapes eleven-year-old Pecola on the kitchen floor.

The narrator tells us of Soaphead Church (Elihue Micah Whitcomb), a self-proclaimed faith healer, whom Pecola asks for blue eyes. He tricks her into poisoning his landlord's mangy dog, then tells her that the dog's death is a sign that her wish will be granted (**SEETHEDOG**).

In **Summer**, Claudia tells us that she and Frieda learned of Pecola's pregnancy by her father from local gossip. First, she is ashamed for her former playmate, then feels only sorrow. According to gossip, only a miracle can save Pecola's baby. Claudia and Frieda intend to help produce that miracle by burying money they have saved near Pecola's house and planting marigold seeds. When the seeds sprout, they believe the miracle that will protect the black baby will happen.

Pregnant and alone, Pecola hallucinates a companion for herself (**LOOKLOOK**). Claudia and Frieda, even her mother, avoid her. The stigma of incest is insurmountable. No longer able to attend school, she embraces the madness that allows her to believe that everyone is only jealous of her blue eyes. She only worries that someone, somewhere, may have bluer eyes than she.

In **So it was.** Claudia recalls seeing Pecola after the baby's premature birth and death, Sammy's leaving, and Cholly's death in a workhouse. Pauline still works for white folks and lives, with Pecola, on a house on the edge of town. Racial self-hatred has destroyed Pecola, still a child, in her desire for love and self-worth. Cholly was the only person who would touch her, and only then in a perverse approximation of love. ❀

List of Characters in
The Bluest Eye

Pecola Breedlove is an eleven-year-old black girl growing up in Ohio. In 1941, before the civil rights movement and the more inclusive paradigm of beauty that has since begun to emerge, she is dark-skinned and coarse featured; considered ugly by black, as well as white, standards. Pecola dreams of having blue eyes—the eyes of white people—and thereby possessing the lenses that would make the world beautiful. She is tormented by almost everyone, yet she never fights back; instead, she imagines ways in which whiteness might be magically achieved. For example, she drinks all she can from the Shirley Temple mug, hoping to ingest as well the icon's blond hair and pink skin. When she is raped by her father and delivers a stillborn child, the black community offers her no comfort, instead scapegoating her for her ugliness and the shame she has brought upon them all. Morrison's story turns on this idea that African Americans too often disdain the outward signs of the racial heritage, what she calls their "funkiness," and hold white racial characteristics to be the beauty ideal. Overwhelmed by her own and the black community's self-loathing, Pecola descends into madness, believing that God has answered her prayers and given her blue eyes. She is a" broken-winged bird that cannot fly."

Claudia MacTeer is Pecola's friend and one of the narrators of the novel. As an adult, she recalls one year in her childhood when her eleven-year-old friend was raped and went mad. She is, in many ways, Pecola's opposite. In contrast to the "broken-winged bird," Claudia, about nine years old in 1941, seems to live up to the promise of the African-American folktale that describes the black angel who learns to fly despite one wing tied behind his back. Given blue-eyed, pink-skinned, white dolls for Christmas, she dismembers them, rejecting the white standards that would label her black and ugly. Claudia is a survivor. Most importantly, Claudia has a strong mother whose love for her daughters is never in question. Because of her mother's strength and example, the MacTeer girls are not brainwashed by the white standards of beauty that even the black community would impose upon them. They will create their own self-worth.

Frieda MacTeer is Claudia's older sister, about ten years old when the events of the novel take place.

Pauline Williams Breedlove, Pecola's mother, resists white standards, refusing to straighten her hair, but has vivid fantasies about movie stars when she and Cholly make love. The pressure to accept white standards of beauty triumphs after Pauline is fired by her white employer and brutally treated by white doctors; she begins to treat Pecola with the same contempt for her dark skin and coarse features. From the time of her birth, Pecola is called only "ugly" by her mother. In contrast, Pauline is the "perfect servant" to the white family for whom she works. (They call her "Polly.") She parrots their white attitudes, even paying more attention to their daughter than to her own.

Cholly Breedlove is Pecola's father. He is an outsider not only to the white community, but to the black community as well. He is the subject of constant gossip, not least because he carelessly starts the fire that burns down the family home. He fails to provide the barest necessities for his family, drinks constantly, fights with Pauline in front of the children, and eventually deserts them. In a chaotic, drunken moment of confused love, he rapes Pecola.

Soaphead Church (Elihue Micah Whitcomb) is a self-proclaimed faith healer. His half-white ancestry, and his Anglo features, please him enormously. By contrast, he finds Pecola's appearance revolting. Gradually, as he realizes that Pecola is too weak to surmount her imperfections, he begins to pity her. He arranges for Pecola to be granted blue eyes in exchange for unwittingly killing a troublesome dog. ✸

Critical Views on
The Bluest Eye

MADONNE M. MINER ON RAPE, MADNESS, AND
SILENCE IN THE NOVEL

[Madonne M. Miner is author of *Insatiable Appetites: Twentieth-Century American Women's Bestsellers*. In this excerpt,
Miner points out the instances in the novel in which male-
female interactions revolve around literal and figurative acts
of rape. She finds a tragic version of the Greek myths of
Philomena and of Persephone in the rape of Pecola.]

Morrison's novel contains repeated instances of Pecola's negation as
other characters refuse to see her. *The Bluest Eye* also provides
numerous instances of Pecola's desire to hide her own eyes, thereby
refusing to acknowledge certain aspects of her world. Morrison
articulates this desire for self-abnegation most explicitly in a post-
script to her description of a typical fight between family members
in the Breedlove home. Mrs. Breedlove hits Cholly with a dishpan,
Cholly returns the blow with his fists, Sammy strikes at Cholly, while
shouting "you naked f——," and Pecola covers her head with a quilt.
The quilt of course cannot completely block out this scene, so Pecola
prays that God will make her disappear. Receiving no response from
the man in the sky, she does her best on her own:

> She squeezed her eyes shut. Little parts of her body faded
> away. Now slowly, now with a rush. Slowly again. Her fin-
> gers went, one by one; then her arms disappeared all the
> way to the elbow. Her feet now. Yes, that was good. The
> legs all at once. It was hardest above the thighs. She had to
> be real still and pull. Her stomach would not go. But finally
> it, too, went away. Then her chest, her neck. The face was
> hard too. Almost done, almost. Only her tight, tight eyes
> were left. They were always left.
>   Try as she might, she could never get her eyes to disap-
> pear. So what was the point? They were everything. Every-
> thing was there, in them.

These paragraphs forcefully convey Pecola's desire and her notion of
how she might realize it. If Pecola were to *see* things differently, she

might *be seen* differently; if her eyes were different, her world might be different too. As Morrison deals out one ugly jigsaw piece after another, as she fits the pieces together to construct Pecola's world, we come to understand the impulse behind Pecola's desire, as well as its ultimate futility. When the boys shout at her, "'Black e mo Black e mo Ya daddy sleeps nekked,'" Pecola drops her head and covers her eyes; when Maureen accuses her of having seen her father naked, Pecola maintains her innocence by disclaiming, "'I wouldn't even look at him, even if I did see him'"; when Maureen attacks her yet again Pecola tucks her head in "a funny, sad, helpless movement. A kind of hunching of the shoulders, pulling in of the neck, as though she wanted to cover the ears." By covering ears, eyes, and nose Pecola attempts to shut out the testimony of her senses. Reminded of her own ugliness or that of her world, she repeatedly resorts to an elemental self-denial.

Pecola quavers when Mr. Yacobowski and Geraldine refuse to acknowledge her. She shrinks in fear when Maureen and Bay Boy insist on acknowledging her ugliness. Quavering and shaking, Pecola does maintain a hold on her world and herself—until Cholly smashes her illusions about the possibility of unambivalent love in this world. Throughout the novel, Pecola ponders the nature of love, pursues it as a potentially miraculous phenomenon. On the evening of her first menstruation, for example, she asks, "How do you do that? I mean, how do you get somebody to love you.'" And, after a visit to Marie, Poland, and China, Pecola ponders, "What did love feel like? . . . How do grownups act when they love each other? Eat fish together?" When Cholly rapes his daughter, he commits a sacrilege—not only against Pecola, but against her vision of love and its potential. Following the rape, Pecola, an unattractive eleven-year-old black girl, knows that for her, even love is bound to be dirty, ugly, of a piece with the fabric of her world. Desperate, determined to unwind the threads that compose this fabric, Pecola falls back on an early notion: the world changes as the eyes which see it change. To effect this recreation, Pecola seeks out the only magician she knows, Soaphead Church, and presents him with the only plans she can conceive. She asks that he make her eyes different, make them blue—blue because in Pecola's experience only those with blue eyes receive love: Shirley Temple, Geraldine's cat, the Fisher girl.

In its emotional complications, Soaphead's response to Pecola's request resembles Cholly's response to Pecola's defeated stance; both men move through misdirected feelings of love, tenderness, and anger. Soaphead perceives Pecola's need and knows that he must direct the anger he feels not at her, but rather at the God who has encased her within black skin and behind brown eyes. But finally, when Soaphead decides to "look at that ugly black girl" and love her, he violates her integrity in much the same way Cholly violates her body when he forces open her thighs. Prompted by the desire to play God and to make this performance a convincing one, Soaphead casts Pecola in the role of believer. Thus, although he sees Pecola more accurately than other characters do, he subordinates his vision of her to his vision of self-as-God. He later boasts in his letter "To He Who Greatly Ennobled Human Nature by Creating It":

> I did what you did not, could not, would not do. I looked
> at that ugly little black girl, and I loved her. I played You.
> And it was a very good show!

Of course, the script for this show sends Pecola into realms of madness. Even Soaphead acknowledges that "No one else will see her blue eyes," but Soaphead justifies himself first on the grounds that "she will love happily ever after" and then, more honestly, on the grounds that "I, I have found it meet and right to do so." In other words, Soaphead's creation of false belief is not necessarily right for Pecola, but for himself. Morrison substantiates this assessment of Soaphead's creation a few pages later, when she portrays its effect on Pecola. Imprisoned now behind blue eyes, the schizophrenic little girl can talk only to herself. Obviously, this instance of male-female interaction parallels earlier scenes from the novel: "rape" occurs as Soaphead elevates himself at the expense of Pecola.

—Madonne M. Miner, "Lady No Longer Sings the Blues: Rape, Madness and Silence in *The Bluest Eye.*" In *Conjuring: Black Women, Fiction, and Literary Tradition,* edited by Marjorie Price and Hortense J. Spillers (Bloomington: Indiana University Press, 1985): pp. 176–189.

[Susan Willis is Associate Professor of English at Duke University. She is author of *Specifying: Black Women Writing the American Experience* and *A Primer for Everyday Life*. In this excerpt, Willis discusses the novel's treatment of the alienation felt by young black women who have come North from the deep South. As they learn "how to behave" according to bourgeois strictures, they learn to repress their spontaneous sensuality, their "funkiness of passion."]

The problem at the center of Morrison's writing is how to maintain an Afro-American cultural heritage once the relationship to the black rural South has been stretched over distance and generations. Although a number of black Americans will criticize her problematizing of Afro-American culture, seeing in it a symptom of Morrison's own relationship to bourgeois society as a successful writer and editor, there are a number of social and historical factors that argue in support of her position. These include the dramatic social changes produced by recent wide-scale migration of industry to the South, which has transformed much of the rural population into wage laborers, the development, particularly in Northern cities, of a black bourgeoisie, and the coming into being, under late capitalism, of a full-blown consumer society capable of homogenizing society by recouping cultural difference. The temporal focus of each of Morrison's novels pinpoints strategic moments in black American history during which social and cultural forms underwent disruption and transformation. Both *The Bluest Eye* and *Sula* focus on the forties, a period of heavy black migration to the cities, when, particularly in the Midwest, black "neighborhoods" came into being as annexes of towns that had never before had a sizable black population. *Sula* expands the period of the forties by looking back to the First World War, when blacks as a social group were first incorporated into a modern capitalist system as soldiers, and it looks ahead to the sixties, when cultural identity seems to flatten out, and, as Helene Sabat observes, all young people tend to look like the "Deweys," the books nameless and indistinguishable orphans. *Song of Solomon* focuses on the sixties, when neighborhoods are perceived from the outside and called ghettos, a time of urban black political activism and general countercultural awareness. And *Tar Baby*, Morrison's most recent book, is best characterized as a novel of the eighties, in which the route back to cultural origins is very long and tenuous, making many individuals cultural exiles.

With this as an outline of modern black history in the United States, Morrison develops the social and psychological aspects that characterize the lived experience of historical transition. For the black emigrant to the North, the first of these is alienation. As Morrison defines it, alienation is not simply the result of an individual's separation from his or her cultural center, although this is a contributory fact that reinforces the alienation produced by the transition to wage labor. For the black man incorporated into the wartime labor pool (as for many white Appalachians), selling one's labor for the creation of surplus value was only half of alienation, whose brutal second half was the grim reality of unemployment once war production was no longer necessary. The situation for the black woman was somewhat different. Usually employed as a maid and therefore only marginally incorporated as a wage laborer, her alienation was the result of striving to achieve the white bourgeois social model (in which she worked but did not live), which is itself produced by the system of wage labor under capitalism. As housemaid in a prosperous lakeshore home, Polly Breedlove lives a form of schizophrenia, in which her marginality is constantly confronted with a world of Hollywood movies, white sheets, and tender blond children. When at work or at the movies, she separates herself from her own kinky hair and decayed tooth. The tragedy of a woman's alienation is its effect on her role as mother. Her emotions split, Polly showers tenderness and love on her employer's child, and rains violence and disdain on her own.

Morrison's aim in writing is very often to disrupt alienation with what she calls eruptions of "funk." Dismayed by the tremendous influence of bourgeois society on young black women newly arrived from the deep South cities like "Meridan, Mobile, Aiken and Baton Rouge," Morrison describes the women's loss of spontaneity and sensuality. They learn "how to behave. The careful development of thrift, patience, high morals, and good manners. In short, how to get rid of the funkiness. The dreadful funkiness of passion, the funkiness of nature, the funkiness of the wide range of human emotions."

—Susan Willis, *Specifying: Black Women Writing the American Experience*. Reprinted in *Toni Morrison: Critical Perspectives Past and Present*, eds. Henry Louis Gates and K. A. Appiah (New York: Amistad Press): pp. 308–329.

DONALD B. GIBSON ON TEXT AND COUNTERTEXT IN THE NOVEL

[Donald B. Gibson is Professor of English at Rutgers University, New Brunswick. His published works include *The Politics of Literary Expression: A Study of Major Black Writers* and *The Red Badge of Courage: Redefining the Hero.* In this excerpt, Gibson points out that the novel's competing narratives show how, though we are oppressed by standards of beauty imposed by the ruling class, we may be instruments of that very oppression.]

The countertextual dynamic of the novel begins with the quotation from the Dick and Jane primer, an introductory gesture, which is in fact and by implication not unlike the prefatory essay to Richard Wright's *Uncle Tom's Children*, "The Ethics of Living Jim Crow" (1938) in that it introduces what is to follow, offers evidence to comment upon and support the thematic implications of the main text, and at the same time informs the main text at each point along its course, its implications engraved within every aspect of plot, character, and description. Morrison's self-consciously epigraphical introduction, the primer text, exists as text and countertext: text in that it has no apparent relation to the major text but lies in the background, the mere genesis of the problem exemplified by Pecola's wanting blue eyes and exemplary, by indirection, of the causes underlying the problematical nature of the lives of the characters in its world; countertext, by turns, in that the epigraphical introduction implies one of the primary and most insidious ways that the dominant culture exercises its hegemony, through the educational system. It reveals the role of education in both oppressing the victim—and more to the point—teaching the victim how to oppress her own black self by internalizing the values that dictate the standards of beauty. "Don't give the girl a fishing pole," the prefatory material tells us, "teach her how to fish," teach her how to enact self-oppression while ostensibly learning to read a simple, unproblematic text. To put this in another way the act of learning to read and write means exposure to the values of the culture from which the reading material emanates. If one wants to read or write, then one must pay for the privilege. The cost of learning to read and write carries with it the necessity to submit to values beyond and other than literacy *per se,* for words do not exist independent of value. One cannot simply learn to read without being subjected to the values engraved in the text.

The introduction to *The Bluest Eye* is also an enabling act, setting up, defining, and effectively writing or reinscribing the nature of what is to be written against. It is the obverse of what in the slave narrative was the act of authentication. Here the author seizes the authority of the authenticator by appropriating and subverting the role of authenticator. That is, the authenticator's role is an authoritative role deriving its authority from socially derived power. The superiority assumed by Charles Sumner and Wendell Philips as authenticators of Frederick Douglass's *Narrative,* for example, is assumed by Morrison herself in her text. Douglass's text is authenticated by Sumner and Philips in the *Narrative* (though he struggles mightily both literarily and historically before wresting away their implied authority). Wright authenticates his own text in "Ethics"; Morrison authenticates her text in the enabling act of her introduction. This is the less complicated aspect of Morrison's discourse in *The Bluest Eye.*

The complications arise when we see that Morrison's sense of the meaning of "bluest eye" is not confined to the meaning we immediately ascribe. The text of the Dick and Jane primer, the epigraphical introduction to Morrison's narrative, is rendered by Morrison in three versions (1–3), each printed in such a way as to appear to grow less comprehensible. The second version omits punctuation, decreasing the space between the lines and running the sentences together; the third omits spaces between the words entirely and arbitrarily breaks words at the end of a line, even words of one syllable. The inference to be drawn is that the final version is incomprehensible. But that is not true. It is, arguably, perfectly comprehensible. The difference between the first and third versions is that the third forces us to participate in the reading in a more active way by demanding that we identify individual words and supply from our own past experience of reading the first version the proper punctuation. The reader is once again, in the very act of reading, taught to read. The meaning is not, as it appears, drained away from first to final draft, but simply concentrated. The implication is that just as Pecola—and all black children—are subjected to the value scheme implied in the primer, so they have imposed upon them whole schemes of value, political, religious, moral, aesthetic, that have little or nothing to do with their actual lives. They are measured using standards they cannot possibly meet—because of genetics and economics—and are found wanting. Yet a paradox arises when we consider that Morrison organizes her text around the primer passage. The sections focusing on Pecola and her family are headed by a line or two from the primer text, the text standing in countertextual relation to the actuality of Pecola's and her family's lives. The final chapter of the novel opens with the primer lines "Look, look. Here comes a friend," and we of course recall that Pecola's friend is hallucinated, the product of her madness. But she does, after all, as the countertext has it, have her blue eyes.

The implication of the novel's structure is that our lives are contained within the framework of the values of the dominant culture and subjected to those values. We have all (there is reason to believe the author does not exclude herself nor anyone else) internalized those values, and to the extent that we have, we are instruments of our own oppression. The text says we are oppressed by the values of the ruling class; the countertext says we participate in our own oppression usually to the extent of being literally the very hand or arm of that oppression.

—Donald B. Gibson, *Toni Morrison: Critical Perspectives Past and Present* (New York: Amistad Press, 1990): pp. 159–174.

LINDA DITTMAR ON THE POLITICS OF FORM IN THE NOVEL

[Linda Dittmar is editor, with Gene Michaud, of *From Hanoi to Hollywood: The Vietnam War in American Film* and, with Diane Carson and Janice R. Welsh, of *Multiple Voices in Feminist Film Criticism.* In this excerpt, Dittmar proposes that meaning, in this novel, is organized dialogically, and that the function of the collective, storytelling act is to make bearable the gulf between childhood acculturation and personal experience.]

That *The Bluest Eye* has been criticized for being mired in the pathology of Afro-American experience is hardly surprising. Violence, madness, and incest are some of the extreme forms this pathology takes here, though the racism which pushes people to such extremes is Morrison's underlying concern. Describing a society where whiteness is the yardstick of personal worth, where Shirley Temple and Jeanne Harlow set standards for beauty and "Dick and Jane" readers prescribe an oppressive notion of normalcy, where Pecola's shame at her mother's race serves as a model for self-improvement, where fathers deny their sons, mothers deny their daughters, and god denies the communal prayer for the privilege of blue eyes—in such a society, Morrison argues, marigolds cannot bloom. The marigolds are metaphoric, of course. The barrenness they signify goes beyond agriculture to include scapegoating and intraracism, "deeply rooted in the primitive history and prehistory of the human struggle with the environment, specifically the struggle for agricultural maintenance symbolized by the seasons and the marigolds."

There are several problems with this metaphor: it leaves the barrenness unaccounted for; it situates social and psychological oppression in the community that receives them (the "soil" in which the seeds were sown); it presents racism as an inescapable atavism; and it provides no means of recovery. In fact, when one surveys the tale of inhumanity *The Bluest Eye* unfolds, it is hard not to question the ideology of its thematics. Readers worry that the microcosm Morrison locates in her Ohio town includes few venues for anger directed beyond the black community and almost no potential for regeneration within it. Read thematically, this novel does indeed seem overwhelmingly pessimistic, given its relentless piling up of abuses and betrayals. Its formal devices partly deflect but never quite extinguish the wish for a plot-based judgment. It is the tension between the two that makes *The Bluest Eye* a problematic novel.

Morrison does not let this tension subside or drop out of view. If anything, this novel's very structure accentuates it precisely because the novel remains inconclusive to the very end. For while *The Bluest Eye* is, indeed, a brilliant orchestration of a complex, multi-formed narrative, the ideological thrust of its structure is ambiguous. Morrison orders her materials into four seasonal parts—autumn, winter, spring, and summer—but within this design nothing is simple or stable. Excerpts from a "Dick and Jane" reader serve as a framing point of reference for Claudia's ostensibly autobiographical narrative; Claudia's account frames Pecola's story; and Pecola's story, in its turn, frames the three long flashbacks which trace the stories of Pauline, Cholly, and Soaphead Church. This elaborate patterning of framing devices attenuates textual accountability. Its mediations deflect attribution, disperse sympathy and identification, and thus question judgment in ways that echo rather than counter the plot's pessimism. They pass on to readers the task of gathering the novel's parts into a signifying whole, even as their ever-shifting modulations of stance assert that the effect is doomed to remain inconclusive.

Inside this Chinese-box arrangement, an obtrusive use of varied typographies further undermines the conventions which normally efface authors' control of their story-telling. Portions of Pauline's narrative are set apart from the rest as oral history; they are italicized first-person accounts which have a distinctly spoken grammar and cadence. Cholly's and Soaphead's narratives are also foreign elements, for they are third-person accounts unattributable to Claudia or any other dramatized narrator. The opening segment in each seasonal division has uneven right hand margins, as does Pauline's narrative in its entirety. While such margins may serve to suggest the text's informal, possibly spoken origins, the mere use of this unusual device is attention-getting, especially given its recurrent suspension and re-introduction. Such intrusion is most noticeable in the "Dick and Jane" passages, where an obtrusive and increasingly unreadable typography emphasizes their role as hostile assaults on Claudia's account. Using "found objects" in apposition to poeticized ones, these passages create an angry dialectic between documentation and fictionality and between the public domain of early childhood acculturation and the private one of personal experience. Numbing the imagination with their simplifications of grammar and life, both the form and the substance of the "Dick and Jane" passages violate the integrity of the life Morrison depicts.

The overall effect of this complexly structured work is to foreground the authorial project of orchestrating a fluid, multi-voiced novel, where the parts sometimes jostle against one another, sometimes complement or blend with each other, and at all times project a dense sense of the multiplicity of narration. Since the function of the story-telling act is, as Claudia puts it, to explain,

Morrison's juxtaposition of diverse voices asserts that under-standing is collective. In this respect, *The Bluest Eye*'s design supple-ments its thematic focus on communities as sites of meaning, for it posits that meanings get constructed dialogically. Maureen Peel and Geraldine, the MacTeers as well as the Breedloves, Mr. Henry and Soaphead Church, the Fishers, Hollywood, and the Maginot Line—these and others collaborate in the production of ideology within the plot. At the same time, *The Bluest Eye*'s very structure parallels the construction of meaning undertaken by its characters. Its shifting points-of-view, flashbacks, and digressions inscribe into the novel's very organization the dialogism evident in its plot. The emphasis here is on understanding and judgment as restless, dynamic, and interactive processes of meaning-production, forever open to modification and change.

—Linda Dittmar, " 'Will the Circle Be Unbroken?' The Politics of Form in *The Bluest Eye*," *Novel: A Forum on Fiction* 23, no. 2 (Winter 1990): pp. 137–154.

TONI MORRISON ON CREATING *THE BLUEST EYE*

[In this extract from the Afterword to Penguin's 1994 edition of *The Bluest Eye*, Toni Morrison discusses the experiences that led her to create the novel.]

We had just started elementary school. She said she wanted blue eyes. I looked around to picture her with them and was violently repelled by what I imagined she would look like if she had her wish. The sorrow in her voice seemed to call for sympathy, and I faked it for her, but, astonished by the desecration she proposed, I "got mad" at her instead.

Until that moment I had seen the pretty, the lovely, the nice, the ugly, and although I had certainly used the word "beautiful," I had never experienced its shock—the force of which was equaled by the knowledge that no one else recognized it, not even, or espe-cially, the one who possessed it.

It must have been more than the face I was examining: the silence of the street in the early afternoon, the light, the atmosphere of confession. In any case it was the first time I knew beautiful. Had imagined it for myself. Beauty was not simply something to behold; it was something one could *do*.

The Bluest Eye was my effort to say something about that; to say something about why she had not, or possibly ever would have, the experience of what she possessed and why she prayed for so radical an alteration. Implicit in her desire was racial self-loathing. And twenty years later I was still wondering about how one learns that. Who told her? Who made her feel that it was better to be a freak than what she was? Who had looked at her and found her so wanting, so small a weight on the beauty scale? The novel pecks away at the gaze that condemned her.

The reclamation of racial beauty in the sixties stirred these thoughts, made me think about the necessity for the claim. Why, although reviled by others, could this beauty not be taken for granted within the community? Why did it need wide public articulation to exist? These are not clever questions. But in 1962 when I began this story, and in 1965 when it began to be a book, the answers were not as obvious to me as they quickly became and are now. The assertion of racial beauty was not a reaction to the self-mocking, humorous critique of cultural/racial foibles common in all groups, but against the damaging internalization of assumptions of immutable inferiority originating in an outside gaze. I focused, therefore, on how something as grotesque as the demonization of an entire race could take root inside the most delicate member of society: a child; the most vulnerable member: a female. In trying to dramatize the devastation that even casual racial contempt can cause, I chose a unique situation, not a representative one. The extremity of Pecola's case stemmed largely from a crippled and crippling family—unlike the average black family and unlike the narrator's. But singular as Pecola's life was, I believed some aspects of her woundability were lodged in all young girls. In exploring the social and domestic aggression that could cause a child to literally fall apart, I mounted a series of rejections, some routine, some exceptional, some monstrous, all the while trying hard to avoid complicity in the demonization process Pecola was subjected to. That is, I did not want to dehumanize the characters who trashed Pecola and contributed to her collapse.

—Toni Morrison, Afterword to *The Bluest Eye* (New York: Penguin, 1994). Reprinted in Toni Morrison's *The Bluest Eye*, edited by Harold Bloom (Philadelphia: Chelsea House Publishers, 1999): pp. 163–167.

LINDEN PEACH ON THE LEVELS OF IRONY IN THE NOVEL

[Linden Peach is author of *Angela Carter, English as a Creative Art, The Prose Writing of Dylan Thomas,* and *British Influence on the Birth of American Literature.* In this excerpt, Peach examines the interplay of ironies arising from the competing narratives of Claudia and the omniscient narrator.]

The text pursues ironies created by the interplay between two levels of articulation in the narrative. One level of articulation arises from the role of Claudia as survivor and her retrospective account of episodes introduced within the context of a season; the other derives from the black kinswoman who narrates the episodes introduced by extracts from the primer. She is an omniscient narrator who is able to provide access to information which Claudia could not have and is able to involve characters outside of Claudia's immediate range of experience. The ironies arising from these two levels of narration are developed within a wider framework provided by the mismatch between what the primer suggests is the norm and the lived experience of the black families.

In discussing the levels of irony within *The Bluest Eye* it is important to remember that Toni Morrison's works are not easily approached through reading habits developed in relation to the realist novel where language often gives the impression of transparency, that is where the representation and the represented are seen as the same thing. In Morrison's novels, language, as the French critic Roland Barthes recognised, is enmeshed with the power structures and forces underlying what we might call 'social reality': 'And the reason why power is invincible is that the object in which it is carried for all human eternity is language: the language that we speak and write.' In Morrison's novels, ideology is not, as envisaged by Marx, an illusion or false consciousness but, as conceived by the French Marxist theorist, Louis Althusser, it is the staple of daily living, embodied in language and in social institutions such as the school, the family and the media.

As we said in the introduction, the dialectic between inherited codes of representation and imagined codes is one of the features which Morrison's work shares with novels from Latin America classified as 'magic realist.' This dialectic emerges in *The Bluest Eye*, as in subsequent novels, from the realisation of the black culture out of which Morrison is writing and of the distortion of the self created by the imposition of white norms on black people. The effect of this imposition is to create a profound sense of fracture. The concept of black in the novel is a construct partly of the characters' own making but mostly social, based on white definitions of blackness which associate it with violence, poverty, dirt and lack of education, whilst Africa is perceived as uncivilised and (negatively) tribal. Black people developed as a social category of low status when Arab trade in African slaves increased, but it was with the European subordination of world peoples as labouring classes that blacks came to form, as McLaughlin says, part of an oppositional and hierarchical system of cultural constructs that justified a coloniser/colonised power system.

In Morrison's novels the struggle to define and create a notion of selfhood in ways which are different from the stereotypical expectations of behaviour carried by the larger symbolic order as whole inevitably involves a process of inner dislocation. As in, for example, *Song of Solomon*, this sense of inner disruption is sometimes resolved positively by the intervention of a female or androgynous figure in the central character's life. But this is not true of Morrison's first two novels where Pecola, suffering from a sense of self-loathing and false identity, retreats into schizophrenia after being raped by her father and where Sula withdraws into her grandmother's room to die alone and unfulfilled.

—Linden Peach, *Modern Novelists: Toni Morrison* (New York: St. Martin's Press, 1995): pp. 24–38.

Plot Summary of
Sula

In the **prologue** to *Sula,* Morrison sets forth the organizing theme and structure of the novel in an ironic inversion of time and social perception. The white social elite's appropriation of the black community of the Bottom follows a circular movement of good and evil, always present and always changing, bulldozing the shacks of the black community to replace them with a sign of civic progress—a country club. The humor and vitality of the black community has been replaced by an orderly, always unsurprising, sign of white status and exclusiveness.

But the reader begins at the Bottom's end, in 1920, already knowing what will happen to that vibrant black community. The black community, the narrator tells us, was remembering and trying to understand what a man named Shadrack "was all about," and what a girl named Sula "was all about." All their narratives are enclosed within the circularity that will lead to the novel's close: "It was a fine cry—loud and long—but it had no bottom and it had no top, just circles and circles of sorrow."

Shadrack's story begins in **1919.** A shell-shocked, twenty-two-year-old World War I veteran, he is released from a veteran's hospital. Confused and damaged, he makes his way home to Medallion, Ohio, and takes up residence in his father's house. Shadrack proclaims the third day of every new year as National Suicide Day. Marching through the community with a cowbell and a noose, he tells his neighbors in the Bottom they may kill themselves or each other. The community thinks he is crazy, but his idea takes hold: "Once the people understood the boundaries and nature of his madness, they could fit him, so to speak, into the scheme of things." Soon, Suicide Day becomes a "part of the fabric of life up in the Bottom"; Shadrack's struggle "to order and focus experience" will be reflected also in the lives of Sula, Eva, and Nel.

In **1920,** Helene Wright, another resident of the Bottom, returns to New Orleans with her ten-year-old daughter, Nel, to see her dying grandmother, Cecile. Until she was sixteen, Helene had lived with Cecile, a woman of strict household and religious convictions.

Rochelle, Helene's mother, was a whore, and Cecile had watched Helene closely for any signs of a similar character. Helene marries Cecile's great-nephew, Wiley Wright (the "Wright" man), and they move to the Bottom to live a respectable and thoroughly conventional life.

On the train, Nel is acutely aware of the contempt she senses in the other black passengers on the train when her mother attempts to ingratiate herself to the boorish and hostile white conductor. Nel observes how the racist degradations and humiliations of the trip South weaken her mother. Nel resolves to be stronger, determined to develop her "me-ness." Cecile dies before Helene and Nel arrive, but Nel meets her grandmother, Rochelle. When Helene and Nel return to the Bottom, Nel befriends a strange and strong-willed girl, Sula Peace.

Eva Peace, Sula's grandmother, is the focus of **1921**. Impoverished and unable to feed her three children, she leaves them with a neighbor and disappears for eighteen months. She returns, prosperous and happy, but missing her left leg. Although the mystery is never solved, the black community suspects that she may have thrown herself under a train in order to collect insurance.

Eva's favorite son, Plum, returns from World War I emotionally scarred, malnourished, and addicted to drugs. Knowing he is doomed to a life of addiction and desperation, she acts with the same desperate and ferocious courage that marked her act to save him when he was a child: Eva rocks him to sleep one night, then soaks his bed with kerosene and sets it on fire. Out of love, she will not allow Plum to die of the decay of his addiction.

The ice cream parlor, in **1922**, seems to contrast Plum's death by fire. Other crises must be met.

Nel and Sula begin their lifelong friendship. Three events shape and strengthen the bond. As the girls walk home from school one day, they are accosted by a menacing gang of Irish Catholic boys. Sula frightens them away when she cuts off the tip of her forefinger. Later, the girls share a metaphorical awareness of their own sexuality as they peel bark from twigs, then rhythmically dig deep holes which they then fill with leaves and cover with earth. Finally, a little boy, Chicken Little, joins them and Sula delights him by swinging him in a wide circle around her. When her hands slip, however, the boy flies into the river and drowns. Sula sees Shadrack on the river bank and runs to him, asking if he had seen what happened to Chicken Little. Shadrack's only comment, "Always," terrifies Sula and she runs to Nel for comfort. The girls tell no one about what really happened to the boy as they sit through his funeral, where Sula cries, but feels no guilt.

Omens, in **1923**, are important to the people of the Bottom. The disturbing disorder they portend centers around Sula's apparent indifference as she watches her mother, Hannah, burn to death. Promiscuous in life, Hannah is mourned in death as a part of the community. She may have slept with everyone's husband but, like Shadrack, the community could understand her: Hannah fit with the natural order of things. But Sula never tried to rescue her mother from the fire. She seemed impassive, just watching. The community will never accept Sula as they did Hannah.

Four years have passed and Nel has married twenty-year-old Jude Green, a waiter at the Hotel Medallion (**1927**). Sula leaves the Bottom and goes to attend college in Tennessee. Unknown to Nel at the time, Sula will not return for ten years.

Part Two, 1937, opens with Sula's return to the Bottom. Immediately following the appearance of a bizarre plague of fifty robins, Sula arrives dressed in movie star fashion, and climbs the hill to the Bottom. She confronts her grandmother, accusing her of Plum's death; Eva recalls Sula's passivity at Hannah's death. Sula terrifies Eva when she threatens to ignite the old woman as she sleeps. By the spring, Sula has made herself Eva's guardian and commits her to a nursing home. The community is shocked—no one commits family to such a place. They are further convinced that Sula is indeed evil. But Nel and Sula are still friends, until Nel finds her with Jude, naked. Now, without either Sula or Jude in her life, Nel is close to despair.

In **1939**, the black community is about to rise up against Sula. In order to see her as the embodiment of evil, they catalogue her transgressions: Her return to the Bottom was marked by the plague of robins; she sent Eva to a nursing home; she watched her mother burn to death; she slept with her best friend's husband. Against what is natural, Sula seems not to age: she loses no teeth; she is never sick; she never belches when she drinks beer. More than these things, though, is that she has shamed them all by sleeping with white men—and she charms Shadrack into tipping his imaginary hat to her as she passes. Outside the community, in a lonely place of "soundlessness," Sula loves Ajax. Ajax loves Sula for her spontaneity and rebelliousness. When she adopts the domestic behavior she had found so appalling in Nel, and begins wearing cologne, Ajax senses marriage on the horizon and leaves her.

Nel, confident in her perception of herself as a "good" woman, goes to visit Sula (**1940**). Three years have passed since Jude left, and she asks Sula why she slept with him. Sula offers no apology, and has no regrets, offering only that Jude "filled up the space." Nel is shocked that Sula did not even love Jude. Sula suggests that, perhaps, Nel cannot discern good from evil, that, perhaps, it is Sula who is good and Nel who is bad. Disturbed by this, Nel leaves her.

Sula, in pain, drifting from the present into the dreamlike past, curls up, fetus-like, on Eva's bed. As she dies, she remembers watching her mother burn, and in her final moment, thinks that she must tell Nel that dying doesn't hurt.

Sula's death is good news for the community, and seems to be associated with new propriety and hope. A new nursing home will be built, which blacks will be able to use; Eva will move into a new home. But, they soon find that, without Sula as community scapegoat, their luck seems to change.

A killing frost and its ice cause wages to be lost when women can't get down the hill to work, the children are sick, and a sense of despair seems to infect the entire black community. Without Sula to compare themselves to, they have no measure of good and evil. Even Shadrack is affected, missing the one visitor he had ever had.

This year's National Suicide Day draws a surprising number and he leads them, dancing and marching, to the tunnel on New River Road. In an hysterical display of both joy and revenge, fueled by years of poverty and the new promise of jobs for blacks at the tunnel, they raid the construction site. Ironically, as if fulfilling the idea of National Suicide Day, the tunnel collapses and many are killed by the wall of water and mud. Shadrack, high on the river bank, watches and rings his bell.

Nearly twenty-five years later, Nel, now fifty-five, remarks how the community has changed (**1965**): "Things were so much better in 1965. Or so it seemed." The narrative has circled back to a time before the prologue. The golf course has not yet been established. The black community of the Bottom has changed. Black people now live in the valley in "separate houses with separate televisions and separate telephones," and no sense of community and family as it had once existed.

Nel's epiphany has been a long time coming. She tells the now senile Eva about Chicken Little's death, and the old woman insists that there is no difference between Sula and Nel, that Nel's watching the boy drown was the same as Sula's watching her mother burn. Later, standing beside Sula's grave, she can no longer deny the perverse evil of her composure watching Chicken Little drown. She and Sula are forever bound together. ❀

List of Characters in
Sula

Sula Peace is Hannah's daughter and Eva's granddaughter. Sula's growing up is marked by the hatred that her community develops toward her. Her friendship with Nel reveals how a strong female relationship can both nurture and cripple female identity. Independent-minded, impulsive, and daring, Sula outrages the black community by sending her grandmother to a nursing home.

Nel Wright Greene is Sula's best friend and the daughter of Helene Sabat Wright. Like her mother, Nel wants a conventional, respectable life. In contrast to Sula, Nel is obedient and cautious, self-sacrificing and determined to hold onto her "me-ness." Nel's friendship with Sula ends when she finds her in bed with her husband, but she forgives her shortly before Sula's death. Twenty-five years later, Nel realizes that, contrary to what she has always held true, it was Sula, and not Jude, who she has missed for so long. The self-knowledge that might have given Nel happiness comes too late.

Shadrack is a shell-shocked World War I veteran who returns home to the Bottom and creates National Suicide Day, to be observed every January 3 by the opportunity to commit suicide without stigma. At the stories end, his role is that of a prophet who leads the townspeople in a ceremony of justice and retribution.

Eva Peace is Sula's grandmother. Although deserted by her husband, she raises three children. A strong matriarch, Eva, apparently out of her great love for her son, kills him rather than watch him deteriorate into mental illness and drug addiction. She is also suspected to have smothered her daughter, Hannah, when she lay dying of burns. Eva is a regal woman, always appearing taller than anyone else. The only person who defeats her is Sula, who assumes guardianship over her and sends her to a nursing home.

Hannah Peace is Sula's mother and Eva's daughter. Beautiful and promiscuous, she sleeps with almost everyone's husband, but has no need to possess any of them. The women of the Bottom like and accept Hannah because she has no desire to take their husbands.

Plum Peace (**Ralph**) is Eva's youngest child and only son. He returns from World War I a weak and defeated alcoholic and drug addict. Eva rocks him to sleep one night and sets him on fire, killing him.

Helene Sabat Wright is Nel's mother. The daughter of a New Orleans prostitute, she does all she can to distance herself from her past. She marries Wiley Wright, moves to the Bottom and builds a conservative, highly respectable life for herself and her daughter.

Jude Greene is Nel Wright's husband. True to qualities suggested by his biblical name, he betrays Nel when he sleeps with Sula, her best friend.

Ajax (**Albert Jacks**) is a friend from Sula's adolescence. He reappears in her life when she is twenty-nine and they become lovers, until Sula's drift into domesticity seems to point to marriage. He runs away. ❀

Critical Views on
Sula

RITA A. BERGENHOLTZ ON THE NOVEL AS SATIRE

[Rita A. Bergenholtz has recently completed a dissertation on twentieth-century satire and holds a Ph.D. from the University of South Florida. She has published articles on Swift, Conrad, Nabokov, and Garcia Marquez. She teaches expository writing and literature at Florida Tech. In this excerpt, Bergenholtz discusses the ways in which Morrison undermines the "binary oppositions" of black and white, male and female, and good and evil, in the novel.]

Morrison employs and undermines binary opposition with the agricultural imagery which she evokes at the outset of *Sula*. The slave in Morrison's "nigger joke" knows what bottom land is, but he is fooled by a "good white farmer" who convinces him that the fertile bottom land is actually up in the hills, which he describes as "the bottom of heaven—the best land there is." The credulous "nigger," therefore, appears to be the butt (or "bottom") of the good white farmer's joke. But is he really? If the Bottom's hilly terrain is unyielding, then why do the white hunters wonder "in private if maybe the white farmer was right after all. Maybe it *was* the bottom of heaven?" And why do the white folks later change their minds, move to the Bottom, and rename it the "suburbs"? Perhaps the knavish farmer is really the fool? In any case, the joke does amuse, for the guileless slave believes—literally—that heaven has a top and a bottom. This brief look at the "nigger joke" which introduces *Sula*—and serves as an emblem for it—highlights a number of binary oppositions that are interrogated throughout the text: black/white, good/evil, tragic/comic, spiritual/material, literal/metaphoric, real/fantastic, and free/enslaved.

Although the introductory joke hinges, in part, upon a black/white opposition, white people remain peripheral figures in this text. Apparently Morrison, like Sula, is not merely concerned with surface differences like color. Plainly, Morrison wants us to understand how reductive and destructive it is to affix antithetical labels such as good and evil to entire races of people, although many of the characters in the novel do just that. For instance, according to the white bargeman who finds Chicken Little's body, black people are simply "animals, fit for nothing but substitutes for mules, only mules didn't kill each other the way niggers did." Similarly, according to most of the residents of the Bottom, the worst thing a black woman like Sula can do is to sleep with a white man: "They insisted that all unions between white men and black women be rape; for a black woman to be willing was literally unthinkable. In that way, they regarded integration with precisely the same venom that white people did." The trenchant irony is not just that both blacks and whites employ binary thinking, but that black women attempt to look more like white women (with all of their nose pulling and hair straightening) and black men yearn to do the white man's work, while both white men and white women, according to *Sula*, secretly lust after black men and their legendary penises. The distinction between black and white is further blurred by the marginal character Tar Baby, a man who may be white or may just be an undefinable mixture of black and white.

Binary thinking operates on the notion that one term of an opposing pair will be privileged. In the following excerpt from an interview, Morrison suggests a weakness in binary perspectives which she explores in *Sula:* "I was interested . . . in doing a very old, worn-out idea, which was to do something with good and evil, but putting it in different terms." Morrison continues: "I started out by thinking that one can never really define good and evil. Sometimes good looks like evil; sometimes evil looks like good—you never really know what it is. It depends on what uses you put it to." Eva, the matriarch of the Peace family and a symbol of black folk wisdom, presents a number of interpretive problems in this area. How, for example, are we to respond to her abandonment of her children, her loss of a limb, and her torching of Plum? Should we admire her stoutheartedness and her ability to survive, or should we be horrified by her actions? What about the deweys? Should we praise Eva's generosity for housing these stray boys or censure her absent-minded treatment of them? Joanne V. Gabbin offers one possible answer when she remarks that Morrison "avoids the pitfalls of attributing all that is good to the tradition. In *Sula* proverbial wisdom of the folk is held up to Morrison's spotlight and collective ignorance often appears." Specifically, Eva follows the folk wisdom which urges a mother to treat her children the same. Consequently, the deweys are "bludgeoned into insipid sameness by folk love and indifference."

Like her grandmother, Sula Peace presents a problem for people who think in binary terms, people who insist that a character be discreet, consistent, and thus confinable. Should we admire Sula's courage, her determination to be free to "make herself"? Or should we loathe her for engaging in casual sex with her best friend's husband? Our initial response to Sula's act of betrayal is to side with the people of the Bottom and label Nel the "good" woman and Sula the "evil" one. After all, Nel behaves properly; she fits nicely "into the scheme of things," into her society's hierarchical structure which has a clear moral top and a definite moral bottom. Indeed, Nel admirably performs all of the obligatory roles: dutiful friend, respectful daughter, loyal wife, and nurturing mother. Later, she acts the wronged wife and the forgiving Christian woman. In contrast, Sula disregards social conventions, following only her own heart and conscience. Sula doesn't care that the definition of a black woman is one who makes other people. Sula doesn't care that the men she sleeps with are married. And Sula especially doesn't care that a "good" woman, like Nel, would never be on top of her man during sexual intercourse but beneath him, not unlike the hem of his garments.

Traditional definitions of satire tend to reduce it to a form of "romance" which, in its broadest sense, may include any narrative which has a well-defined "good guy" who triumphs over a well-defined "bad guy" in order to produce the expected resolution: a happy ending (which is also the moral). Such absolutes, however, are uncommon in satiric novels. In fact, Morrison clearly wants us to recognize that although Nel and Sula appear to be quite different—one the epitome of goodness and the other the embodiment of evil—they are also quite similar. That is, if Sula is evil for watching Hannah dance in pain as flames melt her lovely skin, then Nel is also evil for experiencing a sense of pleasure and tranquility when Chicken Little disappears beneath the water. The "Wright" approach to morality judges an action evil only if it is witnessed by others. In contrast, Morrison suggests that the distinction between good and evil is rarely so clear-cut as Helene and Nel suppose; consequently there is some good and some evil in both Sula and in Nel. The most significant difference between the women might be that Sula accepts the fuzziness of moral categories with her usual good humor, whereas Nel refuses to look at the unacceptable aspects of herself, aspects which confound her clichéd thinking. In fact, Sula's ability to laugh at herself may be her most redeeming quality.

—Rita A. Bergenholtz, "Toni Morrison's *Sula*: A Satire on Binary Thinking," *African American Review* 30, no. 1 (Spring 1996). Reprinted in *Toni Morrison's Sula*, edited by Harold Bloom (Philadelphia: Chelsea House Publishers, 1999): pp. 6–8.

MARIE NIGRO ON THE NOVEL'S MYTHICAL COMMUNITY

[Marie Nigro teaches courses in composition, linguistics, and modern fiction at Lincoln University, where she is also director of the Writing Across the Curriculum program. She has also completed two instructional videos for the PBS series, *A Writer's Exchange*. In this excerpt, Nigro points out that this novel is, after all, a story of community.]

Because *Sula* is the story of a community, the lives of its inhabitants are inextricably interwoven. After the death of Sula—the pariah, the devil, the outcast—the community's role of defining itself through acceptance and disapproval of one of its members shifts. No longer is the she-devil the focus of their collective energies. The misery of the awful winter that follows Sula's death deepens their discontent and stirs up the rage that has lain dormant and without a focus. Shadrack's parade comes on such a bright sunny morning that the townspeople are drawn in a spirit of badly needed camaraderie and fun. Somehow the dancing, laughing parade finds its way to the New River tunnel. The years of frustration, of pent-up anger, become an uncontrollable wave of rage as the marchers hack and hurl at the monument to the White world's refusal to let them in. The violence and tragedy at the tunnel are fitting and ironic because the rage represents a final act of defiance for promises unkept, committed on National Suicide Day, a holiday intended to allay fears of death so that people could get on with their lives.

Early in this article, I noted Wayman's observation that work shapes our lives, and I asked what happens when a person has no work or when a person is forced to engage in work that is demeaning or unsuitable. I also noted Morrison's comment that "Aggression is not as new to black women as it is to white women." In *Sula,* Morrison offers the deadly consequences when the natural feelings of aggression lack a suitable outlet because it is through our work that we define ourselves. Work need not be confined to the concept of earning a living: Work can also be understood as that outlet that allows our creative energies to surface. For Sula, her defiance in refusing to accept demeaning employment or to accept a life prescribed by others may not have been such a tragedy had she had access to an art form with which to express herself. Sula was stubbornly unwilling to define herself as part of the Medallion community and to conform to its standards, and by deliberately placing herself outside of the accepted boundaries, she stood alone. In her quest to "make herself," Sula was following a path that had never been trod before, a path for which she had no tools and no directions. Sula may have succeeded in making herself, but the making process involved pain not only for herself but for all those whose lives she touched.

It is hard to feel sympathy for Jude, the betrayer. We grant him the frustration he must have endured in his job as a waiter, but in seeking a respite from his frustration, he ruins the life of Nel, the wife who was willing to merge her own self into his to allow him to feel like a man.

And finally, we just consider the collective rage unleashed at the tunnel that fateful January 3 on National Suicide Day. Morrison first notes the anger when she describes Jude's humiliation at being turned away from the hiring shack for six days running. It was his need to assuage the rage; it was his determination to take on a man's role that pressed him into settling down with Nel.

And what of the other strong and willing young Black men who were also frustrated by a system that would not allow them to define their manhood through work? The outburst at the tunnel was led by young and enraged men whose audacious acts emboldened the others as they were joined by women and children, smashing the tunnel they could never build.

Morrison points out that there are "several levels of the pariah figure" in her writing. She sees the Black community itself as a pariah community. "Black people are pariahs," she continues. The civilization of Black people that lives apart from but in juxtaposition to other civilizations is a pariah relationship. Morrison explains that although the Black community of Medallion recognized Sula as a pariah, they "thought evil had a natural place in the universe; they did not wish to eradicate it. They just wished to protect themselves from it." The Black community of Medallion allowed Sula to exist as part of the natural order of things. They neither encouraged nor discouraged her as she lived her life; they simply watched and waited.

In *Sula*, Toni Morrison has created an unforgettable story of the friendship of two African American women and has graciously allowed us to enter the community of the Bottom in Medallion, Ohio. More specifically, Morrison has created individual characters and a community of characters whose concept of self has been thwarted by the absence of opportunities for respectable, gainful employment. Sula's lack of an occupation or the absence of clay through which she might express her creative energies denies her the means of defining herself. As desperately as Sula desires to make herself, a racist society will not allow her that opportunity. Similarly, the destruction of the tunnel by the community illustrates the frustration inherent in the consistent refusal of meaningful employment to those who are capable and willing workers but are denied because of their color. Jude's feeling that he is undervalued leads him to a superficial sexual episode with Sula, whose own idleness leads her to engage in meaningless sexual encounters as a means of filling up space in her empty life. Nel's sense of worth is made possible by her acceptance of menial work and her choice to live within the community rather than outside its boundaries as Sula has chosen to do.

By introducing us to the souls who lived and died in the Bottom, Morrison has given us an understanding of social, psychological, and sociological issues that might have been evident only to African Americans. She has lovingly portrayed a mythical community of unforgettable characters now gone forever but not forgotten.

—Marie Nigro, "In Search of Self: Frustration and Denial in Toni Morrison's *Sula*," *Journal of Black Studies* 28, no. 6 (July 1988): pp. 724–738.

[Barbara Christian is Associate Professor of Afro-American Studies at the University of California, Berkeley. Her articles have appeared in such journals as *Women's Studies, Blackworld,* and *Journal of Ethnic Studies.* In this excerpt, Christian analyzes Sula's "freedom of narcissism," and how it allows her to resist the community's confusion of self-hood with selfishness.]

> In a way, her strangeness, her naiveté, her craving for the other half of her equation was the consequence of an idle imagination. Had she paints, or clay, or knew the discipline of the dance, or strings; had she anything to engage her tremendous curiosity and her gift for metaphor, she might have exchanged the restlessness and preoccupation with whim for an activity that provided her with all she yearned for. And like any artist with no art form, she became dangerous.

Sula has the distinction of being herself in a community that believes that self-hood can only be selfishness. Her view of life is different from others, as if the birthmark above one of her eyes has either distorted or enlarged her vision. It is with maddening recognition that we grasp Sula's tragedy—she is too full, and yet too static, to grow. She has stared into that abyss where nothing in life can be relied on—where nothing really matters. Like Cholly Breedlove in *The Bluest Eye,* she has developed the freedom of narcissism allowed only to the gods. Such freedom is not allowed to mere mortals as the oldest stories of all cultures testify. Sula is unique, though, even in the company of mortals who try to live life as if they are divine, for she is a woman. Her life, according to the customs of all traditions, is not hers to experiment with, to create or destroy. Her life is meant to result in other lives. So like Pauline Breedlove in *The Bluest Eye,* she is an artist without an art form. When Sula stares into the abyss that sex so clearly evokes for her, she is not looking for another entity but for another version of herself, for a total union possible only when each perceives the other as possibly being his or her self. Since woman is not usually perceived by man in that total sense, Sula abandons any attempt at union and seeks only herself. Since she cannot have everything, she will at least, or at most, have herself. Marked at birth, she will pursue her own uniqueness.

But such total absorption leads to destructiveness, for the world, used to compromise, will not accept, cannot understand, such concentration—perhaps it must not, to maintain even a slim semblance of order. Using the inexplicable fact that Shadrack is civil to Sula while he shuns everyone else, convinced that she is committing the unforgettable sin—sleeping with white men—and buttressed by her disregard for their God-ordained ways, the town turns Sula into a witch, conjuring spells against her power and acting righteously to prove themselves better than the ignoble she-devil. This lone woman's effect on her community recalls the always perplexing mystery of humanity's need for an evil one, for a devil:

> Their conviction of Sula's evil changed them in accountable yet mysterious ways. Once the source of their personal misfortune was identified, they had leave to protect and love one another. They began to cherish their husbands and wives, protect their children, repair their homes and in general band together against the devil in their midst.

All things have their use and even Sula's evil nature is used by her community to validate and enrich its own existence. As pariah, she gives them a focus through which they achieve some unity, at least temporarily, just as Pecola's madness in *The Bluest Eye* is used by the townsfolk as evidence of their own sanity, their own strength, their own beauty. The need human beings continually exhibit for a scapegoat, so they can justify themselves, is one of the mysteries of human existence that Morrison consistently probes in her works. Why is it that human beings need an enemy, or a martyr, to come together, to feel their own worth, or merely to survive? Why is it that human beings are fascinated with "evil," creating images in its likeness, as children create monsters? It is significant, too, the emphasis the author places on women as accessible scapegoat figures for communities, for any obviously conscious disregard of cultural mores on their part seems to represent not only a threat to the community but to the whole species as well—hence the preponderance of witches, pariahs, and insane women in the history of humanity.

Most importantly, through Morrison's characterization of Eva, Hannah, and Sula, we see that it is not merely social deviance that makes one a pariah. That cursed label is given only to one whose behavior seems so different from, so *at odds with*, the prevailing norm that it cannot be absorbed into the unconscious of the community. In this case, from her birth, the community's unconscious had already been prepared to accept Sula as distinct. It is significant that Sula's birthmark is perceived in different ways, depending on the perspective of the beholder. When Morrison first describes it, "it is something like a stemmed rose" that adds excitement to an otherwise plain face. To Shadrack, who reveres fish, it is the mark of a tadpole, identifying Sula as a friend. To Jude, the mark resembles a rattlesnake, the sting of which is taken away by Sula's smile. To the folk, the mark is Evil, the mark of Hannah's ashes, identifying Sula from her very beginning as a devil. So Sula, not Eva or Hannah, is a pariah because she is distinctly different, because she is consciously seeking to make herself rather than others, and she is totally unconcerned about what others think; in other words, she does not care.

Although Sula does not care about what the community thinks, she does care about Nel, the friend to whom she returns in the Bottom, and she comes to care about Ajax, her lover, for a time. Morrison weaves in a specific pattern the strands of the community's belief system together with the estrangement of Nel and Sula and the love affair of Ajax and Sula so we might better understand the complexity of both points of view. First, the author tells us about the community's view of Nature and Evil, after which we experience the estrangement of Nel and Sula and the community's designation of Sula as a witch. Finally, the story of Sula's and Ajax's relationship is followed by Sula's death and the death of the folk in that tunnel. In carefully charting her pattern, Morrison asks us to contemplate the meaning of her design.

—Barbara Christian, *Black Women Novelists: The Development of a Tradition, 1892–1976* (Westport, CT: Greenwood Press, 1990): pp. 137, 153–175.

[Hortense J. Spillers is Professor of English at Haverford College. She is coeditor (with Marjorie Pryce) of *Conjuring: Black Women, Fiction and Literary Tradition.* In this excerpt, Spillers examines Morrison's description of Sula as a singular "artist with no art form."]

In Sula's case, virtue is not the sole alternative to powerlessness, or even the primary one, or perhaps even an alternative at all. In the interest of complexity, Sula is Morrison's deliberate hypothesis. A conditional subjunctive replaces an indicative certainty: "In a way her strangeness, her naiveté, her craving for the other half of her equation was the consequence of an idle imagination. Had she paints, or clay, or knew the discipline of the dance or strings; had she anything to engage her tremendous curiosity and her gift for metaphor, she might have exchanged the restlessness and preoccupation with whim for an activity that provided her with all she yearned for. And like any *artist with no art form* she became dangerous."

In careful, exquisite terms Sula has been endowed with dimensions of other possibility. How they are frustrated occupies us for most of the novel, but what strikes me keenly about the passage is that Morrison imagines a character whose destiny is not coterminous with naturalistic or mystical boundaries. Indeed the possibility of art, of intellectual vocation for black female character, has been offered as style of defense against the naked brutality of conditions. The efficacy of art cannot be isolated from its social and political means, but Sula is specifically circumscribed by the lack of an explicit tradition of imagination or aesthetic work, and not by the evil force of "white" society, or the absence of a man, or even the presence of a mean one.

Morrison, then, imagines a character whose failings are directly traceable to the absence of a discursive/imaginative project—some *thing* to do, some object-subject relationship which establishes the identity in time and space. We do not see Sula in relationship to an "oppressor," a "whitey," a male, a dominant and dominating being outside the self. No Manichean analysis demanding a polarity of interest—black/white, male/female, good/bad—will work here. Instead, Sula emerges as an embodiment of a metaphysical chaos in pursuit of an activity both proper and sufficient to herself. Whatever

Sula has become, whatever she is, is a matter of her own choices, often ill-formed and ill-informed. Even her loneliness, she says to her best friend Nel is her own—"My own lonely," she claims in typical Sula-bravado, as she lies dying. Despite our misgivings at Sula's insistence and at the very degree of alienation Morrison accords her, we are prepared to accept her negative, naysaying freedom as a necessary declaration of independence by the black female writer in her pursuit of a vocabulary of gesture—both verbal and motor—that leads us as well as the author away from the limited repertoire of powerless virtue and sentimental pathos. Sula is neither tragic nor pathetic; she does not amuse or accommodate. For black audiences, she is not consciousness of the black race personified, nor "tragic mulatto," nor, for white ones, is she "mammie," "Negress," "coon," or "maid." She is herself, and Morrison, quite rightly, seems little concerned if any of us, at this late date of Sula's appearance in the "house of fiction," minds her heroine or not.

—Hortense J. Spillers, "A Hateful Passion, A Lost Love," *Feminist Studies* 9, no. 2 (Summer 1983): pp. 293–323.

MELVIN DIXON ON THE NOVEL'S SHIFTING PATTERNS OF ACCOUNTABILITY

[Melvin Dixon is Professor of English at Queens College, CUNY. His essays on black literature have appeared in scholarly journals and anthologies, including *Chant of Saints: A Gathering of Afro-American Literature, Art and Scholarship*. In this excerpt, Dixon discusses the figuration of land and identity in the novel; how its "geographical images" establish a "theme of moral dualism and double meaning in society and in nature."]

A more complex figuration of land and identity emerges in *Sula*. Beyond the psychological boundaries that imprison Pecola and allow the MacTeer sisters to bear witness to the loss of sexual and mental place, *Sula* tells the story of two women who renegotiate the pressures of place and person through their long friendship, which is not without moments of rupture and discord. The growing bond between Nel Wright and Sula Mae Peace as well as their complementary personalities are first revealed to us by the contrasting features of the land.

Two key terrestrial images frame the novel: the hillside signifying the creation of the black community of Medallion, Ohio, known as the Bottom (through the chicanery of a white planter unwilling to fulfill his promise of valley land to an industrious and newly emancipated slave), and a tunnel under construction at New River Road that collapses upon participants in Shadrack's last march to commemorate National Suicide Day. At first glance, the hillside and the tunnel appear dichotomous. The hillside, or the Bottom, is named ironically, and it is viewed through a passing of time: "there was once a neighborhood." The phrase introduces a narrative about an entire community, but also prophesies its destruction, the hell of mutability alluded to by Nel: "Hell ain't things lasting forever. Hell is change."

One reading of these two regions suggests they have male and female characteristics: the phallic hillside and the vaginal tunnel, particularly when one recalls that the Bottom was established as a black community through a barter between two men. But Morrison gives the two regions feminine traits and infuses them with a preponderance of female properties, in the dual sense. One then suspects a difference personification at work. Irene's Palace of Cosmetology, Reba's Grill, the dance of a "dark woman in a flowered dress doing a bit of cakewalk, a bit of black bottom, a bit of 'messing around' to the lively notes of a mouth organ," all depict a procreative, female environment. The hillside is nurturing; it is a veritable breast of the earth. Within a feminine figuration (accompanying the narrative of a nurturing friendship between Nel and Sula) the hillside complements rather than contrasts with the womblike tunnel, which upon "breaking water" becomes a haunting, unsuspected grave when several Bottom luminaries drown. This "abortion" of life occurs right at the time Medallion is undergoing a kind of rebirth through urban renewal. Whites and blacks are changing geographical spaces: the former moving to the cooler hills, the latter descending to the crowded valley floor. This change and death reverse the notion of economic upward mobility for Medallion blacks, who have only a promise of work on New River Road, and foreshadow the further decline, or bottoming *out,* of the community. The nurture-destruction tension in Morrison's figuration of the land this early in the novel more than prepares us for the complementary relationship, shifting moral dualism, and irony between Sula Mae Peace, who makes and unmakes peace in the community, and Nel Wright, who is never fully as right or as morally stalwart as she would like to appear.

The double figuration of the land as a framing device also foreshadows the novel's curiously double closure. One ending, effected by Shadrack's haunting, successful celebration of death, culminates his search for a "place for fear" as a way of "controlling it" and brings his social marginality to a shocking conclusion. A second ending, however, forces the reader to revise this reading of the novel. Nel's visit to the elderly Eva, now in a nursing home, picks up the unfinished business between Nel and Sula (here represented by Eva) with shattering results: Nel is forced to acknowledge the guilt she shares with Sula for the accidental drowning of Chicken Little who had slipped from Sula's swinging hands and had entered the "closed place of the water." The scene also foreshadows the tunnel's sudden collapse. Nel must also acknowledge the grief for Sula she had tried to suppress, only to discover in her solitary walk home that grief like guilt has no prescribed boundaries; it demands open public expression. When she realizes the extent of her accountability to Sula's friendship—"We was girls together"—Nel lets loose the emotion she had artificially held in check all these years: the cry without "bottom" or "top," but "circles and circles of sorrow." The ever-spiraling geometry of Nel's grief returns readers to the scene of Chicken Little's death and forces us to rethink and replace the event. Sula's "evil" now appears innocuous and Nel's guilt more calculating and malevolent. We must also reconsider Nel's [W]rightness, for her cry admits a moral responsibility for wrongdoing that was not Sula's alone. Riding the spiral of Nel's grief back through the novel, we encounter other geometrical and geographical images that clearly establish the theme of moral dualism and double meaning in society and in nature. *Sula* then becomes as much a novel about the shifting patterns of accountability in Sula and Nel's friendship as it concerns a community's acceptance of moral relativism.

The boomerang effect of the shifting moral and physical geography of Medallion, Ohio, can be seen, for example, in the medallion Sula wears, the birthmark above her eye, the meaning of which changes according to who reads it. Morrison's novel is as much about interpretation as it is about art. How members of the community *read* Sula tells us a great deal about their relation to the land, to themselves, and to the meaning they create. The first indication of this theme is the novel's epigraph, taken from *The Rose Tattoo*, which implicates an entire community, a "they," in the speaker's nonconformist assertion of self: "*Nobody knew my rose of the world but me. . . . I had too much glory. They don't want glory like that in nobody's heart.*" No one really knows Sula or why she sets about—as she tells Eva—to "make herself." But nearly everyone has an opinion about Sula's medallion: a sign they believe of her "evil," her "*too much glory*" in flaunting her disregard of social conventions. At first Sula's birthmark is described as a "stemmed rose"; as she matures, it becomes a "stem and rose," suggesting the duality in nature as well as Sula's developing thorny yet attractive personality. With age, the mark becomes "the scary black thing over her eye." When Jude begins to see the mark as a "copperhead" and a "rattlesnake," he is seduced by Sula. And as Sula becomes the evil the community fears yet abides, her mark indicates either "Hannah's ashes" or, as Shadrack sees it, "a tadpole." No one, not even Nel, knows Sula's heart. Indeed, Sula's closest kin, in terms of the community's social and moral landscape, is none other than Shadrack whose madness makes him at once both an outsider and insider: "Once the people understood the boundaries and nature of his madness, they could fit him, so to speak, into the scheme of things." His shack in the woods or wilderness, halfway between the order of the town and the disorder of the lake where Chicken Little drowned, becomes Sula's refuge, a more useful shelter after the accident than Nel's calculated silence. When Shadrack answers "always" to the distraught Sula's unvoiced question, he seals the doubling of their characters in one word of recognition.

—Melvin Dixon, *Ride Out the Wilderness: Geography and Identity in Afro-American Literature* (Urbana: University of Illinois Press, 1987): pp. 141–169.

Trudier Harris on African American Folk Tradition and the Novel

[Trudier Harris is J. Carlyle Sitterson Professor of English and Chair of the Curriculum in African and Afro-American Studies at the University of North Carolina at Chapel Hill. Her essays on African American literature are widely published. In this excerpt, Harris analyzes the power of folktale in the novel to make the stony "Bottom" seem, instead, the "bottom of heaven."]

As we begin our journey into that other world Morrison has created, we quickly discover a series of reversals: the fantastic events are disturbingly real, and the formula promising wondrous occurrences moves them from the realm of imagination to commonplaces such as war, poverty, and murder. The expected distance collapses, but it does not collapse thoroughly enough for us, without reservations, to accept Shadrack as the guy next door or Sula as the girl next door. Expected dragonslayers become frightened young soldiers afraid of their own hands, afraid that war has taught them not only to kill others but to kill themselves. Ogres are alcohol and drugs, and those strong enough to kill, such as Eva, cannot separate evil from the innocent victims it inhabits. Fires that save Hansel and Gretel or the three little pigs become scars upon the soul of a mother who kills her only son and upon a daughter who quietly watches her mother burn to death.

In another classic Morrison reversal, *Sula* is antithetical to the basic premise of the fairy tale—that the heroine is a helpless, passive creature who must depend upon some man, preferably a stranger, to save her from whatever "fate worse than death" she has innocently or stupidly managed to get herself into. There is little passivity in *Sula*, and innocence is not treasured; indeed, as is typical of Morrison's girl/women, Sula and Nel seem to blossom into adolescence with more knowledge than is comfortable for either of them. In fact, as the experimenter with life, the Ethan Brand type who explores the limits of sin, Sula is an active, destructive artist who, in the absence of "paints, or clay" or a knowledge of "dance, or strings" makes human beings her adventure in life. She is as active as Jack the giant killer and as amoral as Brer Rabbit the trickster.

In this literary folklore, therefore, there is a marked gap between expectation and outcome, between what the familiar leads us to anticipate and what Morrison's changing of the familiar actually provides. She undercuts any potential fairy tale outcomes by making Sula, her princess, a despicable user who needs rescue from no one; by making Eva, her fairy godmother, impotent at the most crucial moment of her life (Hannah's burning); and by making Shadrack, her potential prince, an outcast from the world where his services are most needed. None of these characters portends the "happily ever after" dimension of the formula. By novel's end, the princess is dead, the prince has unwittingly led many of her adversaries to their deaths, the twin sister is almost crazy with grief, and the kingdom is slowly being destroyed.

Its destruction has been foreshadowed in the second structural pattern underlying the novel, the "nigger joke" about the origin of the Bottom. The story fits a classic tale cycle of the black man being duped by the white man:

> A good white farmer promised freedom and a piece of bottom land to his slave if he would perform some very difficult chores. When the slave completed the work, he asked the farmer to keep his end of the bargain. Freedom was easy—the farmer had no objection to that. But he didn't want to give up any land. So he told the slave that he was very sorry that he had to give him valley land. He had hoped to give him a piece of the Bottom. The slave blinked and said he thought valley land was bottom land. The master said, "Oh, no! See those hills? That's bottom land, rich and fertile."
> "But it's high up in the hills," said the slave.
> "High up from us," said the master, "but when God looks down, it's the bottom. That's why we call it so. It's the bottom of heaven—best land there is."
> So the slave pressed his master to try to get him some. He preferred it to the valley. And it was done. The nigger got the hilly land, where planting was backbreaking, where the soil slid down and washed away the seeds, and where the wind lingered all through the winter.
> Which accounted for the fact that white people lived on the rich valley floor in that little river town in Ohio, and the blacks populated the hills above it, taking small consolation in the fact that every day they could literally look down on the white folks.

The tale presents two archetypes of African-American folklore: the white man of means and the "blinking," almost minstrel black man who learns too late the true nature of the bargain he has made. The basic discrepancy inherent in such interactions is also apparent: power (including the language skills to control or create reality) versus the absence of power. The twist in the tale is that the white farmer is the trickster, the figure who dupes instead of being duped.

The story is an etiological one, in that it serves to explain how the current state of affairs came to be. In a world in which the black man is destined to lose, because of or in spite of his labor, the slave here fares no better. The rules of the games will always be changed, as Daryl C. Dance astutely observes in her discussion of etiological tales in *Shuckin' and Jivin'* (1978) and elsewhere; the black man will always receive the reward of lesser value. But Morrison turns the joke around; it is difficult to grow things there, but it is "lovely up in the Bottom," and the trees are so "wonderful to see" that whites speculate on the Bottom indeed being "the bottom of heaven." In spite of their ancestors having been shortchanged, the black folks create reasonably happy lives for themselves in a place almost animate in its influence upon them.

—Trudier Harris, *Fiction and Folklore: The Novels of Toni Morrison* (Knoxville: The University of Tennessee Press, 1991): pp. 52–84.

Plot Summary of
Song of Solomon

The ordinary and the extraordinary, reality and the supernatural, the black community and white "clarification" of meaning collide in **part one, chapter one,** of the novel. Mr. Smith, the black insurance agent, wearing blue silk wings, climbs to the cupola atop the whites-only Mercy Hospital and leaps into the air. In the way incongruous thoughts may settle upon a meaningful unity, we are located on Not Doctor Street, a name settled upon after the post office would not allow the black community to call it Doctor Street. By extension, the hospital at the end of the street is called No Mercy Hospital, since black women were not allowed to give birth inside it—until the day after Mr. Smith's leap. The "clarifying public notice" designating the street Mains Avenue marks the boundary between black and white meaning: Memories may be made stronger by oppression.

Ruth Foster Dead, pregnant, and her daughters, Lena and Corinthians, scurry in the wind to retrieve the velvet rose petals they have stitched to sell to a department store. As the small crowd carefully retrieve what petals they can, Ruth moans, the red petals fly, another pregnant woman bursts into song. Nurses, doctors, and firemen arrive, but "Mr. Smith had seen the rose petals, heard the music, and leaped into the air." The next day, Ruth's son is the first "colored baby" born "inside Mercy."

The wife of Macon Dead, who regards her with contempt, Ruth imagines that, like the gold thread spun by the miller's daughter in Rumpelstiltskin, the milk from her breast nourishes her son as a "golden thread stream from her very own shuttle," long past the age when a child would nurse. Freddie, their janitor and border, discovers Ruth's "secret" and tells the neighborhood. He calls the boy "Milkman,"and the name sticks.

Macon recalls the birth of his son and the appearance, at the same time, of his "bootlegger"sister, Pilate, after an absence of sixteen years. "That the propertied Negro who handled his business so well and who lived in the big house on Not Doctor Street had a sister who had a daughter but no husband, and that daughter had a daughter but no husband. A collection of lunatics who made wine and sang in the streets 'like common steet women!'" His black neighbors see him as an unsympathetic landlord focused upon his account books: "A nigger in business is a terrible thing to see," the elderly Mrs. Bains tells her young grandsons after Macon evicts them.

At twelve, Milkman meets another boy, Guitar Bains. (Guitar and grandmother had earlier been evicted from a house owned by Macon.) Guitar takes him to see Pilate (**chapter two**). The boys are fascinated by this woman with the brass box earring, no navel, and who looks "like a tall black tree." She tells Milkman of the time Macon had saved her life after they had watched their father murdered, blown five feet into the air by a shotgun blast as he sat on a fence. As the boys listen to her stories that seem both true and mythical, Hagar and Reba arrive. Milkman's heroic male quest for his ancestry and it's antithesis in Hagar's demise begin to shape the novel. The women, particularly Pilate, and not the men, will shape his black cultural identity and inheritance.

Freddie tells Macon that Milkman had spent the afternoon "drinking in the wine house." Macon's rage subsides when Milkman resists his anger, reminding Macon of his love and admiration for his own father. "His father had sat for five nights on a split-rail fence cradling a shotgun and in the end died protecting his property," one hundred fifty acres that he had called Lincoln's Heaven. "Maybe it was time to tell him things." But he clarifies nothing for Milkman. On the subject of Pilate, Macon insists that his son stay away from her: "Pilate can't teach you a thing you can use in this world. Maybe the next, but not this one." Macon is to begin working at his father's office after school. Running errands for his father, Milkman has more time to visit Pilate (**chapter three**). At twenty-two, Milkman has been sleeping with Hagar for six years.

Milkman stuns his father one evening by shoving him into the radiator after he strikes Ruth at the dinner table. "Yes, I am my daddy's daughter," she had said with a smirk, somehow provoking her husband's rage. Macon comes to Milkman's room, not to apologize for striking Ruth, but to offer information: "If you want to be a whole man, you have to deal with the whole truth." The truth includes the story of Ruth lying naked on her father's death bed, his fingers in her mouth. She may have been, Macon thinks, more her daddy's daughter than bore thinking about. Milkman considers his feelings for his mother, newly conscious of the shame of being caught nursing at her breast. Her love for him that had seemed natural "now was decomposing."

The day before Christmas Eve, Milkman buys gifts for his parents and sisters (**chapter four**). A gift for Hagar is difficult to find, "since she liked everything but preferred nothing." After twelve years, he is tired of her: "She was the third beer, . . . the one you drink because it's there, because it can't hurt, and because what difference does it make?" He looks for a gift that she might remember him by. He will give her money, and "a nice letter which ended: 'Also, I want to thank you . . . for all you have meant to me . . . I am signing this letter with love, of course, but more than that, with gratitude.'" Hagar is furious. She would kill him in order to possess him.

In **chapter five**, Milkman hides from Hagar in Guitar's room. He also wants to escape everything his father had told him about his mother: In a "mood of lazy righteousness," he reviews what he found out about his mother when he followed her one night as she walked away from home at one-thirty in the morning. She had gone to her father's grave. Waiting for her outside the cemetery, Milkman realized that what his father had told him was true. He cannot understand her. As they return home, Ruth tells her son that her father was "not a good man," but that no one else had ever cared whether or not she lived or died. "I am not a strange woman," she tells him. "I am a small one." She tells Milkman that Macon had tried to kill him, and that he had killed her father by hiding his medicine. Milkman asks her about the description his father had given of her father's death bed. She tells him that she only knelt in her slip at his bedside and "kissed his beautiful fingers." "You nursed me," he accuses. "Until I was . . . old. Too old." "And I also prayed for you," she counters. "What harm did I do you on my knees?"

"Killing, ice-pick-wielding Hagar" wants to murder Milkman. "Luckily for Milkman, she had proved, so far, to be the world's most inept killer." When she has her chance, she cannot kill him. Paralyzed, holding a knife above her head with both hands, Milkman dismisses her by saying, "If you keep your hands just that way, and then bring them down straight, straight and fast, you can drive that knife right smack in your[self]. Why don't you do that? Then all your problems will be over."

Chapter six opens upon Milkman telling Guitar about the near-fatal encounter with Hagar. He accepts no blame for Hagar's distress. Guitar insists, "that girl's hurt—and the hurt came from you." But Guitar has something unexpected to confide. He is a member of a "society" of the Seven Days, who, for every murder, rape, or mutilation of a black man, woman, or child, exacts like vengeance in order to "keep the ratio the same." Milkman insists that many white people are "nice." Guitar counters that they are an "unnatural" race, that "the disease they have is in their blood, in the structure of their chromosomes." Sunday is Guitar's day.

In **chapter seven** Milkman, now over thirty, wants to live on his own, away from his father. He asks him to stake him for a year, and that he will return to work. But Macon wants to teach his son to manage the business. Milkman insists, "Don't do like Pilate, put it [the money] in a green sack and hang it from the wall so nobody can get it." Macon is stunned; he never knew about any sack of money. He tells Milkman of the events that followed the death of the first Macon Dead; how, as penniless children, he and Pilate tried to make their way to Virginia, where they thought they had family. Macon kills an old white man who attacks him in a cave where the children have gone for shelter. They find bags of gold that the man had hidden. Pilate makes him leave it, insisting that, if they are caught, "they'll think that's why we did it." They fight and she threatens Macon with the knife; he waits outside the cave for her. Frightened by approaching men, he runs away, returning days later to find the dead man still there, but the bags of gold gone. "She took it, Macon. After all that, she took the gold." He tells Macon to "get the gold," and that they will split it between them.

Guitar, the Sunday man, prepares to arrange the deaths of four white girls to approximate that of the four little colored girls who had been killed in the explosion of a church (**chapter eight**). In his waking dreams, "scraps of Sunday dresses" remind him of the pieces of red velvet that Lena and Corinthians had caught "under the gaze of Robert Smith," who was also a member of the Seven Days. Milkman tells him about the gold, offering to split it three ways if Guitar will help to get it. With the money, he can buy the explosives and materials necessary to arrange the killings. Plotting the theft with Guitar, Milkman "could look forward to both fun and fear"—and freedom. In the night, the moon shining like a flashlight into

Pilate's window, they steal the sack of gold. At another window on the same side of the house, a woman wonders, "What the devil they want that for?"

In **chapter nine**, in 1963, Corinthians has been for two years a maid for the State Poet Laureate, Michael-Mary Graham. Ruth and everyone else believe her to be the woman's amenuensis. A Bryn Mawr education and a year in France have "unfit her for eighty percent of the useful work of the world," and Corinthians must keep her education a secret from her employer.

On the bus home, Corinthians meets Henry Porter, a handyman who has occasional work in the white neighborhood. She goes to his room in a house owned by her father. The story circles back to an earlier time, when Macon had come to collect rent from this same Henry Porter who had "screamed, wept, waved a shotgun, and urinated over the heads of the women in the yard" (**chapter one**). Like Guitar, he is a member of the Seven Days.

Macon, Milkman, and Guitar have discovered that the sack taken from Pilate's house contains only rocks and human bones (**chapter nine**). Macon surmises that, if Pilate took the white man's bones, then the gold must still be in the cave. Milkman and Guitar listen as Pilate tells Macon that she had returned to the cave not for the gold, but for the bones of the dead man. "I went cause Papa told me to. . . . [I]f you take a life, then you own it. You responsible for it. . . . [T]he dead you kill is yours."

Milkman's journey to the cave is marked by an encounter with Reverend Cooper, who tells him about the shotgun murder of the first Macon Dead, and stories of his family that he had heard all his life but which, here, weave his life into a greater narrative (**part two, chapter ten**). He discovers that there had been two sets of bones in the cave—one of the man he killed, and one of their father, whose body had been dumped there by the white men who shot him. The bones he had stolen from Pilate belonged to their father. Convinced that she had taken the gold, too, Milkman follows her path to Shalimar, Virginia. In Shalimar, he seeks his "original home," the place from which his grandparents had come (**chapter eleven**). Guitar has followed Milkman into the South, thinking he has already found the gold and means to keep it all for himself (**chapter twelve**).

Chapter thirteen returns to Hagar, in Guitar's room, the moment just after Milkman left her still holding the knife. Guitar guesses that "neither Pilate nor Reba knew that Hagar was not like them. . . . She needed what most colored girls needed: a chorus of mamas, grand-mamas, aunts, cousins, sisters, neighbors, Sunday school teachers, best girl friends, and what all to give her the strength life demanded of her—and the humor with which to live it." She believes that Milkman's antipathy toward her is because she in no way measures up to the American ideal of beauty, her hair least of all. Hagar's death seems inevitable.

In **chapter fourteen**, Milkman hears the story of Solomon, or Shalimar, the "flying African." In **chapter fifteen**, he can hardly wait to return home to tell his father and Pilate that his "great-grand-daddy" had flown back to Africa, and that the town, Shalimar, is named after him. But Guitar still hunts him for the nonexistent gold. "Everybody wants a black man's life," he thinks, even black men. "Would you save my life or would you take it? Guitar was exceptional. To both questions he could answer yes."

Pilate greets him by knocking him out cold with a bottle. She throws him into the cellar. He tells her about her father's bones, and that the dead man wants her to bury him "where he belongs. On Solomon's Leap." She lets Milkman leave—with a box of Hagar's hair.

Macon is uninterested in the story of Solomon / Shalimar. "No reconciliation took place between Pilate and Macon, and relations between Ruth and Macon were the same and would always be. Just as the consequences of Milkman's own stupidity would remain, and regret would always outweigh the things he was proud of having done. Hagar was dead and he had not loved her one bit. And Guitar was . . . somewhere."

Milkman returns to Shalimar with Pilate to bury her father's bones. Guitar shoots her at the burial site; Milkman, holding her, sings to her as she dies. He then shouts to Guitar, "You want my life? You need it? Here." And "he wheeled toward Guitar and it did not matter which one of them would give up his ghost in the killing arms of his brother. For now he knew what Shalimar knew: If you surrendered to the air, you could *ride* it." ✹

List of Characters in
Song of Solomon

Milkman Dead is the male protagonist of the novel. He journeys out of spitirual death into understanding and responsibility, his liberation symbolized by his discovery of the secret, mythical power to fly like his great-granddaddy, Solomon (or Shalimar). Milkman must choose between the fierce materialism of his father, Macon Dead, and his Aunt Pilate's sense of history and family. He becomes a complete human being in the process of realizing a mythic, spiritual power—and his African-American identity.

Ruth Foster Dead is Milkman's mother, and the daughter of the doctor for whom Not Doctor Street is named. After caring for her father, alone, until his death, she marries Macon Dead. She manages her household with "guileless inefficiency," and terrible cooking. Her relationship with her father still troubles Macon, and his suspicion that theirs was an unwholesome affection has destroyed his desire for her. Ruth, in turn, out of her powerlessness, provokes him to violence. Her deepest love was for her son, forever called Milkman after she is discovered nursing him long past the age when it is thought appropriate.

Macon Dead is Milkman's father and Ruth's husband. He is a prosperous landlord and land speculator who has some trouble reconciling his respectability with the fact of his women relatives who live a seemingly chaotic life in a small house just outside of town. He dominates the lives of his wife and children. In pursuit of a white ideal of business success, the pleasures of black community are lost to him. He wants his son to follow him into business.

Lena Dead and **First Corinthians (Corrie) Dead** are Milkman's older sisters. Corinthians has a Bryn Mawr education and had spent a year in France, leaving her overeducated and too refined for even her most upwardly mobile peers. In her forties, she takes a job as maid to a celebrated woman writer, but tells Ruth that she is an "amanuensis." Eventually, she finds some happiness with one of her father's tenants.

Pilate Dead, Macon's older sister and Milkman's aunt, is a boot-legger and magical healer who shares a house with her daughter and granddaughter. Pilate's appearance is distinguished by the absence of a navel, and by the brass box, containing a paper with her name on it, that dangles from one earlobe. She saved Milkman from the abortion Macon tried to force upon Ruth, and she is with him at his spiritual coming of age at the end of the novel.

Hagar is Reba's daughter and Pilate's granddaughter. She and Milkman are lovers for many years, until he tires of her. Hagar thinks that her appearance has driven him away. She cannot meet the American standard of beauty, and her efforts to do so are a sad failure. The quality of her hair troubles her most. The intensity of her grief at losing Milkman turns violent; she would rather kill him than lose him.

Reba is Pilate's daughter and Hagar's mother. She is reknowned for her good luck. That is, she wins or finds anything she pays attention to. Like Hagar, she associates love with possessiveness and gift-giving.

Guitar Bains is Milkman's friend. He is a member of the Seven Days, a secret group of black men who exact vengeance upon whites for crimes committed against blacks. After four little colored girls are blown up in a church, he is to blow up four little white girls in like manner. This requires money for explosives; he follows Milkman in search of gold supposedly taken by Pilate many years before. ✾

Critical Views on
Song of Solomon

WILFRED D. SAMUELS ON THE DEPTH OF THE NOVEL'S
MALE CHARACTERS

[Wilfred D. Samuels is Associate Professor of English and Ethnic Studies at the University of Utah. His articles and essays have appeared in *Black American Literature Forum, Callaloo, Umoja: Scholarly Journal of Black Studies,* and *Explicator.* He is author of *Five Afro-Caribbean Voices in American Culture, 1917–1929,* and co-editor of *"Our Spiritual Strivings": Recent Developments in Afro-American Literature and Criticism.* In this excerpt, Samuels observes how Milkman, Porter, Macon, and Guitar represent a new complexity in Morrison's male characters.]

With her treatment of Milkman as the protagonist, Morrison offers a more in-depth treatment of the black male character than, with the exception of Shadrack, has been heretofore witnessed in her work. Through her characterization of Milkman, we are given a better rounded view of and careful insights into the complexity of the black male, his aspirations, frustrations, and determination. Morrison confessed that her effort here was intentional; she wanted to look at the world from a man's point of view: "I've never considered looking at the world and looking at women through the eyes of men [before]. It fascinated me. It really was, for me, the most incredible thing in the world. I was obsessed by it . . . I mean trying to feel things that are of no interest to me but I think are of interest to men, like winning, like kicking somebody, like running toward a confrontation; that level of excitement when they are in danger." Morrison accomplishes much of this task through the salient friendship and camaraderie that Milkman and Guitar share, but also through the other men. Here, unlike in *Sula,* for example, the men are not superficial or immature; Porter, Macon, Milkman, and Guitar are in fact most complex.

In Porter's story, for example, we see that men, too, can be desperately alone and lonely. That he has a need for more than physical love is suggested in the subtle allusions that make him a Christ figure. He is laden, like Jesus, with a love for humanity, hence the significance of the name "Porter." "I love ya all . . . I'd die for ya, kill for ya. I'm saying I love ya . . . Oh God have mercy," he tells a crowd that mocks him much as Christ was mocked while on the cross. He acknowledges the congruence of their experiences when he states: "You [Jesus] know all about it. Ain't it heavy?" The implications are related not solely to the difficulty involved in loving one's fellowman but also to doing so unselfishly, without the expectation of reciprocity. This quality is lacking in black male/female relationships, Morrison seems to have concluded in her previous assessments. Porter's unselfish love is responsible, in the end, for Corinthian's resurrection from the "Dead," from the meaningless world of materialism of her father's home.

Morrison's treatment and characterization of Macon Sr. is equally significant. Although we may not approve of his actions, we are given ample information to understand the source of his behavior. This does not lead to justification but to empathy. We feel the depth of Macon's loneliness and emptiness, for example, in the poignant image of this ostensibly powerful man hiding in the dark outside Pilate's house. For a brief moment we are drawn into the chaos within him. More important, Macon does not abandon his family, as Boy-Boy does. Although we may conclude that he perceives them as his possession, we must acknowledge that the territorial instinct is also present. He seems willing to guard and protect that which is his, in spite of his inability to openly show affection.

The intricacy of Morrison's black male characters is seen, however, in the special friendship that develops between Guitar and Milkman. It is akin to that which developed between Nel and Sula, in that there seems to be reciprocity until, through misunderstanding, one experiences betrayal. These men also differ from Nel and Sula in that they are independent of each other, each complete within himself. Nevertheless, like Pilate, to whom he introduces Milkman, Guitar serves as mentor; he is a friend "wise and kind and fearless." Above all, Guitar seems to be a surrogate father, replacing Macon, whom Guitar does not resemble in any way. Milkman considers Guitar "the only sane and constant person" in his life. He finds sanctuary in Guitar's home as well as a willing listener and an understanding friend in his more experienced comrade. Guitar shows sensitivity to Milkman's confusion when he tells him, "Looks like everybody's going in the wrong direction but you, don't it?," at the point that Milkman was thinking about his inability to conform. He encourages Milkman to assume the responsibility for his own life. "You got a life? Live it!" he tells him.

In spite of his admirable qualities, however, Guitar is potentially dangerous, as his membership in the Seven Days, a vigilante group, suggests. He lacks not only Pilate's shamanistic powers but, more important, her spirit of forgiveness and love for humanity. Like Macon II, he harbors and is enslaved by a deep hatred of whites as a result of his father's brutal death at the hands of whites. The degree to which this hatred becomes a destructive force for Guitar is manifested when he joins the Seven Days. Insecure and paranoid, he is unable to trust anyone, even his devoted friend. When Macon evicts Guitar for back rent, he holds Milkman responsible and considers it a breach of their friendship. Desperate for money, he agrees to accompany Milkman on his search for the lost gold, but believing that Milkman is "not being serious," he is not trusting. He tells Milkman, "I'm nervous. Real Nervous." Convinced that he has been betrayed by Milkman, whom he believes does not intend to uphold the agreement to share the buried gold, Guitar stalks him to kill him. Paradoxically, he reveals his intention to kill Milkman. When Milkman asks why he has chosen to tell him, Guitar responds, "You're my friend. It's the least I could do for a friend."

Guitar seems honest in his response: He is torn between commitment to his friendship and his membership in the Seven Days, his only apparent source of a sense of place. Ironically, in counseling Milkman, Guitar has told him that everyone has desired his life. Now, it becomes obvious that *everyone* is indeed all inclusive, for it includes his best friend. In the end, Milkman makes the ultimate sacrifice and gives his life to his friend: "You want my life?" he asks Guitar, "You need it? Here." Consequently, even here there is a paradox, for in the final moment between the two, Milkman experiences triumph when he learns the ultimate sacrifice: "Not love, but a willingness to love," by unselfishly giving oneself to mankind, by meeting the challenge of his friend-become-nemesis, Guitar.

—Wilfred D. Samuels, "Liminality and the Search for Self in *Song of Solomon*," *Minority Voices* 5 (Spring–Fall 1981): pp. 59–68.

STEPHANIE A. DEMETRAKOPOULOS ON THE NEEDS OF HAGAR'S FEMININE TYPOLOGY

[Stephanie A. Demetrakopoulos is Professor of English at Western Michigan University. She is author of *Listening to Our Bodies: The Rebirth of Feminine Wisdom* and articles on a variety of subjects in the fields of literature, women's history and consciousness, and Jungian psychology. In this excerpt, Demetrakopoulos examines the ways in which Hagar and the other women of the younger generation "explode out of the [feminine] niches others have made for them."]

While Lena and Corinthians have had to deal with the bitterest faces of the masculine—a cruel father, an indifferent brother, and a literal killer-lover (for Corinthians)—their cousin Hagar has had an insulated and pampered childhood. The sisters have grown strong enough (although warped) in coping with the harsh reality of their home life.

As Guitar so astutely notes, Hagar's feminine typology needed a traditional community of women to help her reach adulthood. Hagar does not want to be unattached and floating like Reba and Pilate; Morrison says that at age twenty-three she dreams of a Prince Charming who will change her life. She has grown up completely surrounded by a chaotically feminine yet providing world. She has never had to strive for anything. Like Sula she has never had to carry any responsibility; she apparently does not work although she does help with the wine making sometimes. She is able to spend her life drifting because Pilate and Reba see themselves as the providers for her. They obviously love her to distraction as seen in her funeral when they sing her back to themselves, internalize her as their baby, their "sugar lumpkin." But for all the poignancy of this matriarchy's tender love for its own, still Hagar is dead. Ironically, their totally uncontingent and supportive love may have taken from her the development of strength she needed to survive Milkman's abandoning her. Also missing in her life are male relatives to help build her animus, her sense of the way to deal with men; when Pilate tries to make her see Milkman as a cousin/brother, Hagar immediately seduces him. She sees him as one more gift from her mothers for her self-indulgence. As he gains maturity, she projects the total numinosity of the masculine onto Milkman, making him carry the divine animus, her soul. Without him she feels she will lose her grounding in the feminine world, in the world itself even. She is like Sula vis-à-vis Ajax.

For Hagar, time is only cyclical, tied to feminine rhythms; she cannot comprehend the irrevocable passage of linear time. She is ruled by the moon, her hair standing up like a thundercloud on the thirtieth day of each menstrual cycle when she attempts to kill Milkman. Hagar is at age thirty-six still a girl; she has not tracked the irrevocable linear passage of time and cannot believe that she has given nineteen years of her life to Milkman and that he can write her off. She thinks that she can metamorphose back into a perfect young girl like Cinderella through a mad shopping trip in which she pathetically dons all the Madison Avenue clichés. She tries for rebirth by simply changing her exterior, her persona. When Guitar finds her on her last murder attempt, she sits holding her breasts like rejected fruit, sensing herself as the barren yet vegetative feminine.

Because Hagar has been so pampered, she does not really know how to assert herself except by murdering the demonic and rejecting masculine or by repackaging her body. She has been terribly "over-mothered," calling both Reba and Pilate "Mother"; and Pilate beats her, a thirty-six-year-old woman, when she tries to kill Milkman. Everyone in the community sees her as the two women's daughter. She is trapped in a Persephone/Kore role that has reduced her to a Baby Bear or Goldilocks slot within her family. She has absolutely no resilience. She and Sula are the tail ends, the remnants of a purely matriarchal line that has no connections to the masculine world. Hagar looks like Pilate and reflects Pilate's creative energy in the wild growth of her hair; but she does not have Pilate's strength for going it alone. Hagar's hair is a metaphor for the wild and chaotic feminine in her that has no form, no institution like that of a traditional marriage or a role in her community (like teacher, nurse, doctor) into which it can flow. She dies close to the advent of middle-age, dolled up like a young girl. This is no particular person's fault by any means; in fact, Hagar's mothers have had only good will towards her. But by totally protecting Hagar as a symbol of the future of their line, as their baby, Pilate and Reba may have unwittingly participated in her destruction. Three other elements are at least as present in her demise: her own temperament, Milkman's cynical indifference towards her, and the commercial values of American culture. Yet I think the aspect most missing in her is the strength that comes to women from the ardor of either raising children or working to support oneself. Sula dies the same way as Hagar, and when an author tells us the same pattern twice, we should believe she means it.

In these women of the younger generation—Lena, Corinthians, and Hagar—Morrison uses life-stage boundaries to delineate character change and growth. The women explode out of the niches others have made for them, individuating in bent and killing ways, but nevertheless insisting on change. Their explosions further Milkman's individuation; he has, as his father's delegate, tried to force Corinthians to give up Henry Porter—but she escapes. Then Lena tells him of his selfishness. Hagar kills herself and Pilate gives Milkman Hagar's hair, saying that he must carry his guilt.

Part of Milkman's ego death is a self-crucifixion when he realizes how selfishly he has treated Pilate and Ruth when only these two old women have really cared for him. As Pilate dies in his arms in the conclusion, she instructs him about *caritas*, love of all humans, his oneness with the cosmos. Milkman realizes her lesson on grounded-in-relatedness flying; he knows now how to construct a true self and a good life too. He leaps to wrestle his own shadow, the nihilism and narcissism of Guitar. He has already won.

> —Stephanie A. Demetrakopoulos, "The Interdependence of Men's and Women's Individuation." In *New Dimensions of Spirituality: A Biracial and Bicultural Reading of the Novels of Toni Morrison* by Stephanie A. Demetrakopoulos and Karla F. C. Holloway (Westport, CT: Greenwood Press, 1987): pp. 85–99.

HARRY REED ON THE MOTHER / SON CONFLICT IN THE NOVEL

[Harry Reed is author of *Platform for Change: The Foundations of the Northern Free Black Community, 1775-1865* and *Studies in the African Diaspora: A Memorial to James R. Hooker.* In this excerpt, Reed analyzes how Milkman's indifference to the sacrifices his mother, Ruth, has made for him leads her to a new assertiveness and sense of self.]

While Milkman is central to the resolution of the dense thematic thrust of *Song of Solomon*, his quest is buttressed by his female relationships. The fluid constellations of black women loving him, supporting him, guiding him and even rejecting him confirm the nurturing aspects of black life. Milkman is generally unconcerned about his effect on the females in his life. He neither knows about nor cares about the sacrifices they make to keep him whole and healthy. He accepts without question his mother's protection, but he cannot reciprocate when she needs support.

> Milkman leaned against a tree and waited at the entrance. Now he knew, if he'd had any doubts, that all his father had told him was true. She was a silly, selfish queen, faintly obscene woman. Again he felt abused. Why couldn't anybody in his whole family just be normal?

As Morrison shows, Milkman neither realized nor cared that he was the most recent in a long line of men who had oppressed her.

Ruth's father, Dr. Foster, had never approved of his future son-in-law, Macon Dead. Later he refused to give Macon a loan to complete a business deal. Macon, in turn, never forgave his wife for siding with her father. He also resented his wife's seeming distaste for sex, but the final straw in his rejection of her was the scene he witnessed between her and her dead father. Later Macon relates that story from his male perspective to his son. Even Ruth's handyman perceives of her as weird and then circulates stories about her.

Through all of the refracted male views of Ruth, none of the viewers pauses long enough to listen to her. Even her son—reflecting on his own sense of betrayal—does not understand her explanation. What she describes is her oppression by the black males in her life, not the oppression of an undefined white power structure. People she expected to love her, to accept her and to nurture her had not, as she explains to her son.

> . . . Because the fact is that I am a small woman. I don't mean little, I mean small, and I'm small because I was pressed small. I lived in a great big house that pressed me into a small package. I had no friends, only schoolmates who wanted to touch my dresses and my white silk stockings. But I didn't think I'd ever need a friend because I had him. I was small, but he was big. The only person who ever really cared whether I lived or died. Lots of people were

interested in whether I lived or died but he cared. He was not a good man, Macon. Certainly he was an arrogant man, and often a foolish and destructive one. But he cared whether and he cared how I lived, and there was, and is, no one else in the world who ever did. And for that I would do anything. It was important for me to be in his presence, among his things he used, had touched. Later it was just important to know he was in the world. When he left it I kept on reigniting that strange cared-for feeling that I got from him. I am not a strange woman. I am not a strange woman. I am a small one.

Poignant as it is, Ruth's story evokes Milkman's interest only when she mentions his Aunt Pilate. His attention then is only momentary: he is more concerned about asking "Were you in the bed with your father when he was dead? Naked?" "No," she answers, "but I did kneel there in my slip at his bedside and kiss his beautiful fingers. They were the only part of him that wasn't. . . . " Milkman cuts her off and hurls the accusation "You nursed me." When Ruth answers in the affirmative Milkman then asserts "Until I was . . . old, too old." His indictment is answered with chilling force from Ruth:

And I also prayed for you. Every single night and every single day. On my knees. Now you tell me. What harm did I do you on my knees?

For the moment the question is lost on Milkman. Like the other men in her life, Ruth's son is convinced that she is indeed a strange woman.

Had Morrison left Ruth at this point it would have been just another example of the Madonna/bitch theme that the work of so many male nationalist writers perpetuates. The Madonna/bitch theme illustrates the ambiguity that black males feel for mothers and wives, but especially mothers. Conflicts inherent in the theme are exacerbated when the black male attempts to gain autonomy *vis-à-vis* the white power structure. A standard resolution of this tension is the black male's condemning of the love and protection of the black female, possibly because she has diverted his attention from confronting whitey and denigrated his manliness by suggesting what he sees as cowardly alternatives.

Morrison offers a different and more compelling resolution of the mother-son conflict. First, any attempt to reach an immediate mediation dissolves. Milkman has had his biases corroborated and so fails to comfort his mother. Second, telling the story triggers the remembrance of Pilate's support. And it is this other black female who helps Ruth begin to shape her life and to shed her smallness. Thus Morrison opens new views of black life by incorporating black woman's quest for selfhood, autonomy, and growth. Ruth begins to assert herself, not in a domineering way but with newly discovered ego-strength. Significantly her new assertiveness is not structured to educated black males about their shortcomings, or to castrate them for them. Instead she works on behalf of other black women.

Equally important, she begins to identify once more with Pilate, her sister-in-law. Initially they are drawn together because of Ruth's son, Macon, (she refused to call him Milkman) and Pilate's granddaughter, Hagar. Several years older than Milkman, Hagar refused to accept his ending of their relationship. She had indeed made several inept attempts to kill him. Ruth warns Hagar to leave her son alone. Unseen by Ruth or Hagar, Pilate listens to each say why she is important to Milkman. Pilate puts both of their relationships to him in the proper perspective by noting, "He wouldn't give a pile of swan shit for either one of you."

—Harry Reed, "Toni Morrison, *Song of Solomon* and Black Cultural Nationalism," *The Centennial Review* 32, no. 1 (Winter 1988): pp. 50–64.

MICHAEL AWKWARD ON THE TRAGIC IRONIES OF THE NOVEL'S MALE EPIC

[Michael Awkward is Associate Professor of English at the University of Michigan, Ann Arbor, where he also teaches in the Center for Afro-American and African Studies. He is author of *Inspiring Influences: Tradition, Revision, and Afro-American Women's Novels* and editor of *New Essays on "Their Eyes Were Watching God."* In this excerpt, Awkward examines Milkman's coming to terms with Solomon's "cele-brated act of flight" from social responsibility and the female left behind.]

Morrison's delineation in her novel of feminist concerns is perhaps most clearly evident in the (predominantly) female voices of descent that operate in a censurous chorus in the last chapters of *Song of Solomon*. Shalimar females such as Susan Byrd and Sweet are, by and large, remarkably unimpressed by Solomon and by his transcendent act. Susan Byrd, in fact, openly criticizes him for his desertion of Ryna and his offspring. While Byrd recounts to Milkman the provocative aspects of Solomon's mythic flight—she tells Milkman, "according to the story, he . . . flew, like a bird. Just stood up in the fields one day, ran up some hill, spun around a couple of times, and was lifted up in the air. Went right on back to wherever it was he came from"—her narrative focuses primarily on the pain felt by others as a consequence of his desertion. Indeed, it is Susan Byrd who informs Milkman of the derivation of the name Ryna's Gulch: "sometimes you can hear this funny sound by [the gulch] that the wind makes. People say it's the wife. Solomon's wife, crying. Her name was Ryna." In addition to censurious assertions such as "he disappeared and left everybody," she comments further on the rami-fications of his leave-taking flight:

> "They say she screamed and screamed, lost her mind com-pletely. You don't hear about women like that anymore, but there used to be more—the kind of woman who couldn't live without a particular man. And when the man left, they lost their minds, or died or something. Love, I guess. But I always thought it was trying to take care of children by themselves, you know what I mean?"

While we might rightly question here the reliability of Susan Byrd's "speculations"—for instance, the song of Solomon is no mere, negligible "old folks' lie"; further, Hagar's response to Milkman's desertion is of a kind with Ryna's, and her grief clearly has nothing to do with the difficulty of single parenthood—certainly the reader can trust her recollections of the particulars of the mythic narrative. That the reader should trust her view of the magnitude of the deserted female's pain is confirmed by the reac-tions of Sweet and, ultimately, of Milkman, to male acts of aban-donment and transcendence.

Milkman's archaeological act fills him with an "incredible high" under whose influence he relates to his Shalimar lover Sweet the fact that he is a descendent of Solomon. Having taken possession of his familial history—he asserts proudly of the ring shout that accompanies the recitation of the song of Solomon, "It's my game now"—he says of his forebear: "The son of a bitch could fly! You hear me, Sweet? That motherfucker could fly! Could fly! He didn't need no airplane. Didn't need no fuckin tee double you ay. He could fly his own self!" Unimpressed by the knowledge of Milkman's royal heritage—after all, as Susan Byrd tells him, "everybody around here claims kin to him"—Sweet tries to force her lover to consider the consequences of Jake's transcendent act by asking, "Who'd he leave behind?" Still mesmerized by his status as descendent of such a magical figure, Milkman giddily responds: "Everybody! He left everybody down on the ground and sailed on off like a black eagle." It is only when he is forced to confront the consequences of his desertion of Hagar that he is capable of sensitivity to the socially irresponsible nature of his ancestor's actions, and, further, of his own.

Such confrontation occurs when, upon his return to Michigan, Milkman is exposed to male flight's significant, sometimes deadly, consequences. Recovering in Pilate's cellar from a blow by his justifiably angered aunt which had rendered him unconscious, Milkman comes to understand the tragic ironies of a phallocentric social (and narrative) structure which fails to permit female access to the culture's sources of knowledge and power. The narrative informs us of Milkman's revelations: "He had left her. While he dreamt of flying, Hagar was dying." Milkman, who, despite his infinite leap in knowledge, clearly still has much to learn, then recalls Sweet's question about the victims of Solomon's departure, a question which he had not seriously pondered previously. He begins to see a clear connection between his act and that of his mythic forebear, the full impact of whose flight he can now understand:

> Sweet's silvery voice came back to him: "Who'd he leave behind?" He left Ryna behind and twenty children. Twenty-one, since he dropped the one he tried to take with him. And Ryna had thrown herself all over the ground, lost her mind, and was still crying in a ditch. Who looked after those twenty children? Jesus Christ, he left twenty-one children! . . . Shalimar left his, but it was the children who sang about it and kept the story of his leaving alive.

It is only at this point, when he learns the painful consequences of the celebrated male act of flight, that Milkman's comprehension of his familial heritage and the song of Solomon can be said to move toward satisfying completion. Such understanding requires coming to terms with his familial song's complex, sometimes unflattering meaning, and acknowledging both its prideful flight and the lack of a sense of social responsibility in the mythic hero Solomon's leave-taking act.

Song of Solomon, then, is a record both of transcendent (male) flight and of the immeasurable pain that results for the female who, because of her lack of access to knowledge, cannot participate in this flight. In breaking the monomythic sequence, Morrison provides the possibilities for a resistant feminist reading which suggests the consequences of male epic journeys: the death-in-life, or actual death, or the female whose only permissible role is that of an aggrieved, abandoned lover.

Thus, an analysis that foregrounds not only Milkman's archaeological question, but also Hagar's disintegration—in other words, an afrocentric feminist reading of *Song of Solomon*—allows for an interpretation that most closely suggests the complexity of Morrison's appropriation of the epic form and the Afro-American folktale. Such an analysis is necessary, in fact, if we are to comprehend the black and feminist poetics which inform not only *Song of Solomon,* but the author's entire corpus. Rather than reinventing patrimony, Morrison's novel affirms the timeless relevance of the myth's insistence on the importance of transcendent flight as implicitly phallocentric in their inscription of a perpetually inferior—non-"heroic"—status for the female.

Morrison's male epic does not represent a break with the female-centered concerns of works such as *The Bluest Eye* and *Sula,* but is a bold extension of these concerns in a confrontation with the tenets of Western literature's most "sacred narrative" form. Like Guitar, who insists that he has earned the right to censorous analyses of the actions of Afro-Americans, Morrison's text asks, in effect, "can't I criticize what I love?" While she dearly wishes to preserve the wonder and wisdom of black culture, Morrison perceives the need to invest the preserved forms of culture with "new information." If cultures generally are not static but are in the process of continual and dynamic development, clearly Afro-American culture, if it is to be valuable in the present as a means of explaining a rapidly changing world in which women are increasingly important and influential actors, cannot continue to produce perspectives which lead to the further creation of narratives that trivialize or marginalize the female. Such recognition does not mean a replacement of afrocentric ideology with feminism, but the creation of spaces that will allow for their necessary and potentially fruitful interaction. In that sense, *Song of Solomon* not only reflects the perspectives of Afro-American culture, but seeks to contribute in significant ways to its transformation.

> —Michael Awkward, "'Unruly and Let Loose': Myth, Ideology, and Gender in *Song of Solomon*," *Callalloo* 13, no. 3 (Summer 1990): pp. 482–498.

DOREATHA DRUMMOND MBALIA ON MILKMAN'S RISE TO RACE AND CLASS CONSCIOUSNESS

[Doreatha Drummond Mbalia is author of *Heritage: African American Readings for Writing* and *John Edgar Wideman: Reclaiming the African Personality*. In the excerpt, Mbalia introduces the first of three developmental stages by which Milkman's underdeveloped race and class consciousness will become an understanding of people that will permanently alter his view of women.]

By the time she writes *Song of Solomon*, Morrison seems fully conscious of the relationship between the individual African and his community. Evidently, after writing and considering the dilemmas presented and the solutions posed in *The Bluest Eye* and *Sula*, after witnessing and participating in the historic, valiant struggle waged by Africans in the sixties and early seventies, and after being in contact with and editing the works of conscious, revolutionary Africans such as Chinweizu, Morrison has become more aware of the dialectical relationship between capitalism, racism, and sexism. In *Song of Solomon*, she subordinates sexism to both racism and capitalism, realizing that the exploitation of the African woman by the African man is the result of his national and class oppression. That is, sexism is correctly viewed as the consequence of the African's lack of race and class consciousness. Morrison's awareness of these relationships empowers her to create a protagonist whose survival depends on his development of a people consciousness, which, once gained, permanently alters his view of women. One has only to contrast Milkman's relationship with Hagar and Sweet to appreciate the veracity of this statement. After *Song of Solomon*, Morrison will never again create a male protagonist whose race and class consciousness is so underdeveloped that he exploits and oppresses African women.

In fact, this work marks a qualitative leap in Morrison's consciousness as an African and as a writer (for her, the two are inextricably related) in several other regards: she is more aware of the importance of dialectical and historical materialism; she is more aware of the role capitalism plays in the African's exploitation and oppression; she is more aware of the need to create a protagonist who develops during the course of the novel; and she is more aware of the importance of creating a text that allows theme to dictate structure.

To fully appreciate the qualitative leap that Morrison makes in regard to the nature of the African's oppression in the United States and in regard to her artistic dexterity, her protagonist's growth should be viewed as three distinct yet interconnected developmental stages that lead to his increased race and class consciousness: the preliminal stage, the liminal stage, and the postliminal stage. There are general characteristics peculiar to each as well as particular characteristics associated with the protagonist's heightened consciousness.

In the opening chapters of the novel, Milkman's low level of consciousness in regard to his people's race and class oppression manifests itself in his nickname. Ironically, Macon Dead III acquires it as a result of his extended nursing period, for instead of helping him to become more attuned to his mother and her needs, this lengthy bonding period proves ineffectual in a society that promotes selfish individualism above love and concern for humankind: Milkman is emotionally estranged from Ruth Dead as he is from all women with whom he interacts. As his nickname suggests, he milks women, pilfering their love and giving nothing in return. Even at age thirty-one, he knows very little about women, an ignorance made evident by his inability to distinguish his sisters from his mother. Nor can he conceived of women as human beings, not even his mother: "Never had he thought of his mother as a person, a separate individual, with a life apart from allowing or interfering with his own." Women, in general, have value only as "need providers" for Milkman. Therefore, his act of urinating on Lena becomes an act symbolic of his pissing on all women, Hagar in particular.

It is Hagar who is most exploited. While she genuinely loves Milkman, he loves her solely as a receptacle in which to empty his lust, seldom taking her anywhere except the movies and considering her his "private honey pot." Eventually, even sex with her becomes a bore, being "so free, so abundant." So, as a pimp taking leave of his whore, Milkman pays Hagar for twelve years of service and writes her a thank you letter, reminding her that they are first cousins and self-righteously telling himself that he is performing a selfless act. Like Sula, Milkman—in this liminal stage—shits on those around him, particularly the women of the novel.

Pilate is no exception. From her, as from Hagar, he receives a love both free and abundant. Wallowing in it, Milkman feels for "the first time in his life that he remembered being completely happy." Most important, it is because of Pilate—the pilot—that he is steered in a conscious direction. Through her acknowledgement of, dignity in, and proudness of her Africanness, despite her lack of material wealth, Milkman gets his first lesson in race and class consciousness: "While she looked as poor as everyone said she was, something was missing from her eyes that should have confirmed it." Like Pilate, Milkman must learn to respect his African self and to realize that money does not ensure happiness. Instead of killing the potential savior of his people as does her biblical namesake, Dead Pilate breathes life into Milkman. It is she who first forces him to confront his identity as the living dead who sucks the life force from his people; from her he learns the essence of life. Devouring the fruity, yolky core of life and speaking in a voice that reminded Milkman of little round pebbles that bumped against each other, Pilate is nature personified. She is, in fact, earth mother. What Milkman gives her in return for life is the murder of her daughter and the theft of her father. Significantly, it is not until the Shalimar Hunt, when he learns the importance of whispering to the trees and the ground, touching them, "as a blind man caresses a page of Braille, pulling meaning through his fingers," that Milkman appreciates the life that this earth mother provides him.

It is quite apropos, in light of his surname, that Milkman at first reciprocates Pilate's love with death. Like all the members of the Macon Dead household, he is dead. Even the family car, a spotlessly clean Packard, is regarded by the community as a hearse, a car that cauterizes the ties between the living (the community) and the dead (the Dead family). As the community voice of the novel, the Greek chorus, Freddie's evaluation of the Dead is valid: "A dead man ain't no man. A dead man is a corpse." At this point in his life, Milkman Dead is neither a man (exploiting all women with whom he comes into contact), nor a human being in general. He is both psychologically and emotionally dead.

> —Doreatha Drummond Mbalia, "*Song of Solomon:* The Struggle for Race and Class Consciousness." Reprinted in *Toni Morrison's Song of Solomon,* edited by Harold Bloom. (Philadelphia: Chelsea House, 1999): pp. 126–128.

JAN FURMAN ON MILKMAN'S HEROIC QUEST

[Jan Furman is editor of *Slavery in the Clover Bottoms: John McCline's Narrative of His Life During Slavery and the Civil War.* In this excerpt, Furman proposes that Milkman's quest is not that of the classical hero, for fortune or honor. As a contemporary black man lost to his community, family, and to himself, his quest is for his humanity.]

In many ways Milkman's journey from his home in Michigan to Pennsylvania to Virginia and back home conforms to the classical male monomyth of the heroic quest. In this structure the hero's adventure takes him on a journey beset with mortal danger but a journey which, in the end, brings him nobility and great honor among his people. Of course, Morrison does not faithfully, nor with a straight face, appropriate the monomyth paradigm to her own story and character. She admits that *Song of Solomon* is her "own giggle (in Afro-American terms) of the proto-myth of the journey to manhood." She feels that "whenever characters are cloaked in Western fable, they are in deep trouble." One kind of trouble is the customary designation of male narrative as more imperative than female narrative. Morrison would, no doubt, decline to identify her novel with a narrative tradition so antithetical to her aesthetic, which makes her consistently attentive to women's narratives even in a text like *Song of Solomon*, which is primarily devoted to men's experiences. Instead, then, of blithely conceiving Milkman's journey in terms of the traditional hero's, Morrison satirically calls attention to the limitations of the traditional quest by making Milkman less heroic and more human. Not a classical hero, Milkman is a contemporary black man lost to his community, family, and, most important, lost to himself. His true quest is not for fortune or honor but for his humanity.

Every phase of his search for gold brings Milkman closer to these truths. In Danville, Pennsylvania, Fred Garnett, a passing motorist, teaches Milkman that not everyone is motivated by financial gain. When Milkman offers him money to pay for a Coke and a ride from the country into town, Garnett shakes his head in disgust and disbelief. Milkman learns that one man can give another "a Coke and a lift now and then" without expecting payment. Reverend Cooper's stories about "old Macon Dead," Milkman's grandfather, about Lincoln's Heaven, the farm that he worked and loved, about the old man's son, Macon Dead, Jr., who "worked right alongside" his father, reveal for the first time to Milkman the powerful balm in the phrase, "I know your people!" As he listens to the old men's recollections of the past, "He glittered in the light of their adoration and grew fierce with pride." These experiences in Danville begin to unravel Milkman's webbing of indifference just as the difficult country terrain where he searches for gold spoils the superficial finery of his clothes. By the time he returns to town, Milkman has experienced, in the river stream where he loses his balance and falls in, the first baptismal to a new life. His three-piece suit and Florsheim shoes are soiled and torn, hs "heavy over-designed." watch is splintered, the minute hand broken as if to signal an eruption. In the country he comes face to face with his limitations. "He had no idea that simply walking through trees, bushes, on untrammeled ground could be so hard. Woods always brought to his mind city parks, the tended woods on Honore Island where he went for outings as a child and where tiny convenient paths led you through." But here Milkman is alone, far from a town, in a place where his father's money is irrelevant. Here he must chart his own course. And that course must be one that takes him away from old paths of insolence, greed, and vanity toward new paths of spiritual enlightenment. Milkman still has far to travel. The journey so far has brought him to an appreciation of family and hard work that he did not have before, but buried treasure continues to make a slave of him. He does not yet know that money cannot buy the kind of freedom he needs.

This insight is not available to Milkman until the second phase of his journey in Shalimar, Virginia. Pilate may have gone there, he thinks, and buried the gold. In this small southern community with no commerce or industry, what is left of Milkman's flashy affluence is insolent to the people who live there: his casual willingness to simply buy a car to replace the broken one he bought the day before, the insult of locking his car against the men he has asked for help, calling them "them," not bothering to give his name or ask theirs. "He was telling them they weren't men . . . that thin shoes and suits with vests . . . were the measure." The possum hunt, however, that Milkman is goaded into joining changes all of that. Finally, stripped of everything except his watch (and he will soon lose that), dressed in brogans, army fatigues, and a knit cap, Milkman, like the other hunters, must take his measure against the laws of nature. Survival depends upon penetrating the darkness, transversing the rocky terrain, interpreting the dogs' barks, anticipating his prey, sending wordless messages to his companions.

—Jan Furman, *Toni Morrison's Fiction* (Chapel Hill: University of South Carolina Press, 1996): pp. 34–48.

Plot Summary of
Beloved

Chapter one, introduces the motifs that will shape the major themes of Toni Morrison's *Beloved:* Allusions to numerology and bestiality; the presence or absence of color; the natural world that may simultaneously reflect beauty and horror; the reciprocal bond between mother and child in breastfeeding and the mammary rape of Sethe; the iron that symbolically infuses Sethe's eyes and back with strength; the supernatural; and resurrection, both in the "dawn-colored stone studded with star chips" on Beloved's headstone and in the profane challenge of the dead child's return to Sethe.

The haunted house at 124 Bluestone Road, near Cincinnati, Ohio, is "spiteful" and "[f]ull of a baby's venom." In 1873, Sethe and her daughter, Denver, are all that remain of a once close family that included Grandma Baby Suggs; Sethe's two sons, Howard and Buglar; and her infant daughter, Beloved. Nine years earlier the boys had been driven away by the ghost and, shortly after, Grandma Baby Suggs died, "with no interest whatsoever in their leave-taking or hers." Mother and daughter try, without success, to work a truce with this ghost who responds by moving the furniture.

The abrupt arrival of Paul D Garner, a "Sweet Home Man," interrupts the solitude of Sethe and Denver. Sethe tells Paul D about the events that caused her to run from Sweet Home; about sending her sons and daughter north without her; about the white boys who stole her breast milk and then whipped her back raw; about the "whitegirl," who helped her survive and birth Denver; and about the death of her baby girl. They talk about their life in slavery under the kindly Garners, and the coming of the cruel overseer, known only as "schoolteacher," after the death of Mr. Garner. Sethe asks Paul D to stay. The ghostly light and sense of sorrow he feels from it convince Paul D that Sethe and Denver should move out. Sethe replies, "I got a tree on my back and a haint [a ghost] in my house, and nothing in between but the daughter I am holding in my arms. . . . I will never run from another thing on this earth." She begins to think that, perhaps, she could "[t]rust things and remember things because the last of the Sweet Home men was there to catch her if she sank."

But Sethe and Paul D are both dissatisfied with their sexual encounter: "His dreaming of her had been too long and too long ago (**chapter two**)." The tree on Sethe's back that "whitegirl" had likened to a chokecherry tree now seems to him "a revolting clump of scars"; her breasts he could "definitely live without." Sethe and Paul D lie quietly together, each with their own memories of slavery: Paul of his slave-brother Sixo; Sethe of Mrs. Garner's kitchen, of her selection of Halle from among the male slaves and their six-year marriage, and of Halle's crippled mother, Baby Suggs.

The novel's circular narrative draws also upon other impressions: "Denver's memories were sweet (**chapter three**)," accompanied by the sensuous pleasure of cologne and the canopy of the boxwood hedge where, hidden and private, she may "stand all the way up in emerald light." Exhausted by loneliness, Denver retreats to this shelter to ponder the "magic" of her birth and the puzzle of Sethe's scant memories of her own mother, known only as Ma'am. The voices of mother and daughter blend to retell the story of Sethe's ordeal after fleeing Sweet Home and of the cruel "schoolteacher." Saved from death by a sixteen-year-old indentured servant, Amy Denver, Sethe gives birth to Denver and the two women wrap the baby in rags on the riverbank before Sethe escapes across the river into Ohio. Inside the house Paul D sings prison songs as he repairs the broken furniture. He remembers "working like an ass" in the prison quarry and "living like a dog," but worse was "the box built into the ground" that had done him the favor of "[driving] him crazy so he would not lose his mind."

Paul D takes them to a carnival (**chapter four**). Images of violence and sensory confusion begin to shape the novel's tone: As roses die, their scent becomes "louder"; the white circus people astonish them by "eating glass, swallowing fire, spitting ribbons, twisted into knots, forming pyramids, playing with snakes and beating each other up." Late that afternoon Paul D, Sethe, and Denver return from the carnival to find a wet, exhausted woman resting in front of 124; she introduces herself as Beloved.

Beloved hovers like a "familiar" around Sethe, waiting for her when she returns from work and up before her every morning (**chapter six**). Beloved gets a "profound satisfaction" from Sethe's storytelling, but the retelling of events hurts Sethe "like a tender place in the corner of her mouth that the bit left." A recurrent motif is in the power of human touch to heal and give comfort: Sethe grooms Denver's hair and answers Beloved's questions about her mother and the branding mark by which she was always to know her. As if an omen, a bit of Denver's hair thrown into the fire "explode[s] into stars" and Sethe, startled, recalls "something she had forgotten she knew." Her wet-nurse, Nan, had told Sethe stories in an African language she has forgotten: Sethe is the only child her mother, "taken up many times by the crew" on the slave ship, had not "thrown away."

Paul D reveals that Halle had been in the barn when the boys had taken Sethe's milk from her, and that it had broken him (**chapter seven**). In reaction he had scooped butter from a churn and smeared it on his face. Rage replaces Sethe's love for Halle as the memory fills her mind of "two boys with mossy teeth, one sucking on my breast the other holding me down, their book-reading teacher watching and writing it up," and Halle "looking and letting it happen." Paul D recalls his own humiliation under the gaze of the rooster, Mister, the proud witness to his degradation, as he stood chained, with a bit in his mouth: "[W]asn't no way I'd ever be Paul D again, living or dead. Schoolteacher changed me. I was something else and that something was less than a chicken sitting in the sun on a tub." Sethe responds with soothing comfort, massaging his knee—"Nothing better than that to start the day's serious work of beating back the past."

In **chapter eight**, Beloved describes a place that suggests both the womb and the grave—or Hell. She tells Denver she has "come back" only to be with Sethe, that "She left me behind. By myself." Denver responds by "construct[ing] out of the strings she had heard all her life a net to hold Beloved," telling her the story of her birth to then nineteen-year-old Sethe. Her monologue becomes "a duet as they lay down together, Denver nursing Beloved's interest like a lover whose pleasure was to overfeed the loved."

Religious conventions and the need for a ritual treatment of the past permeate **chapter nine**. Sethe blames herself for Baby Suggs' death, twenty-eight days after her arrival; she "knew the grief at 124 started when she jumped down off the wagon, her newborn tied to her chest in the underwear of a whitegirl looking for Boston." Memory returns Sethe to the riverbank where she waits, "alone and weak, but alive," with her baby, seeking a way to cross. She finds herself "near three colored people fishing—two boys and an older man," Stamp Paid, and his two sons. Stamp ferries Sethe and Denver across the Ohio River and hides them at safe house (on the Underground Railroad). A young woman, Ella, brings news that Stamp had safely brought her three children to 124 Bluestone. Looking at Sethe's newborn child Ella muses that it's best not to love anything.

In **chapter ten** more details emerge about the death of Beloved. Denver recalls her brief education at Lady Jones' school which ends when a curious boy makes clear to her why they are shunned: "Didn't your mother get locked away for murder? Wasn't you in there with her when she went?" Denver never returns to the school.

In **chapter eleven**, Beloved gains emotional power over Paul D. She seduces him "with empty eye," promising to leave only if he will touch her "on the inside part" and call her by her name. Act merges with dream as he reaches "the inside part" and awakens, calling out "Red heart. Red heart. Red heart." Denver is also seduced by Beloved (**chapter twelve**). She imagines the attentions of a sister in the uncritical gaze of Beloved. Denver is certain that Beloved is 124's ghost, but she seeks only for ways to please Beloved and to keep her close.

Paul reflects on life under Mr. Garner at Sweet Home as Morrison deftly frames the paradox of benign slave ownership (**chapter thirteen**): "He thought what they said had merit, and what they felt was serious. Deferring to his slaves' opinions did not deprive him of authority or power. It was schoolteacher who taught them otherwise. A truth that waved like a scarecrow in rye: they were only Sweet Home men at Sweet Home. One step off that ground and they were trespassers among the human race." Paul D tells Sethe that he has been overpowered by Beloved and, to reclaim Sethe, his manhood, and to escape Beloved's control, he suggests that they conceive a child.

In **chapter fourteen**, Beloved reasserts her power over Sethe in a repulsive, infantile act: She pulls out a tooth with her thumb and forefinger. In an unusual revelation—and a departure from the narrative—we know Beloved's thoughts. The pulled tooth, she thinks, presages her doom. She cannot remember "when she first knew that she could wake up any day and find herself in pieces . . . she thought it was starting." It is Beloved's only circumspect moment.

We return to Baby Suggs and her memory of a day when the "four [white] horsemen," symbols of the Apocalypse and signs of famine, war, pestilence, and death, arrive at 124 Bluestone (**chapter sixteen**). Schoolteacher, one of his nephews, one slave catcher, and a sheriff have come to take Sethe—and her children—back into slavery. Sethe cuts the infant Beloved's throat and tries to kill her two sons and Denver. As the sheriff takes Sethe into custody, she holds Denver to the nipple and the child swallows both milk and Beloved's shed blood. In a shocking juxtaposition, a white boy hands Baby Suggs a pair of shoes and demands they be repaired: "[Mama] says you got to have these fixed by Wednesday," and Baby Suggs replies dully, "I beg you pardon. Lord, I beg you pardon. I sure do." (It is worth considering here the thoughts of writer Jamaica Kincaid who recently asked how history might have been different if slaves had not embraced Christianity as their religion.)

In **chapter eighteen**, Sethe admits to Paul D that she had been jailed for murdering Beloved: "I stopped [schoolteacher]," she tells him, "I took and put my babies where they'd be safe." Paul D thinks that "[t]his here new Sethe didn't know where the world stopped and she began. . . . "Your love is too thick," he tells her. "Love is or it ain't," she replies, "Thin love ain't love at all." Proof that her love "worked" is that her children "ain't at Sweet Home. Schoolteacher ain't got em."

Chapter twenty-two contains one grammatical statement: "I am Beloved and she is mine." In the mind of the dead child sensory impressions yield images without logic or syntax, and they suggest her existence among the dead. She resists death only because of her love for Sethe, insisting "I am not dead I am not." **Chapter twenty-three** also begins "I am Beloved and she is mine." But, here, the language seems more earthly, and an interrogatory dialogue between mother and daughter merges with Denver's voice.

In **chapter twenty-six**, Sethe has become obsessed with Beloved and the tensions at 124 and loses her job. Beloved takes "the best of everything." Sethe, losing her sanity, and Beloved, getting fatter by the day, are at war with each other. Denver turns to Lady Jones for maternal warmth and a job away from 124. Edwin Bodwin, the Quaker abolitionist who had provided the house for Baby Suggs and her family, hires Denver as a night nurse. As he arrives in his cart, Sethe, remembering the arrival of schoolteacher in a cart eighteen years earlier, runs at him with an ice pick.

Here Boy, the family dog who disappeared when Beloved arrived, returns in **chapter twenty-seven**, marking the departure of Beloved who "some say, exploded right before their eyes." Sethe again becomes whole (**chapter twenty-eight**). Memories fade and they forget Beloved "like a bad dream." ❀

List of Characters in
Beloved

Sethe (b. 1835) is a survivor of slavery. At age thirteen, she is brought to Sweet Home, an idyllic Kentucky plantation owned by the kindly Garners. Within a year, she has chosen Halle as her "husband" and, by age eighteen, has born three children. When a brutal overseer takes charge, Halle and the rest of the "Sweet Home men" attempt to escape, and Sethe sends her children to Ohio on the Underground Railroad, planning to follow them later. The bitter memory of boys holding her down and taking her breast milk; the brutal lashing afterward; her flight and Denver's birth; all is soothed by Baby Suggs when Sethe at last reaches Cincinnati. When the overseer comes to reclaim her and her children under the Fugitive Slave law, Sethe cuts the throat of her oldest daughter and attempts to kill the others, and is condemned to hang. She gains release and returns to the house at 124 Bluestone Road. After the death of Baby Suggs, she lives in solitude with Denver and the ghost of her murdered infant daughter, Beloved. The arrival of Paul D eighteen years later presages the ghosts departure and Sethe's emotional healing as their narratives interweave and they make their stories one.

Beloved (1854–1855) is Sethe's infant daughter and Denver's older sister, murdered by Sethe to spare her from slavery. She is the venomous baby, the "almost crawling? baby," and the Beloved of the title. She haunts 124 Bluestone Road as a spirit and as a young woman who clings to Sethe like a vengeful familiar, seduces Paul D, and manipulates Denver. Beloved is reified (thing-ified) anguish not containable by Sethe's narrative, a living presence, a manifestation of Sethe's rage and helplessness.

Denver (b. 1855) is Sethe's eighteen-year-old daughter. Solitary and imaginative, she clings to the preternatural and malicious Beloved as a sister and companion. Born during Sethe's flight from Sweet Home to Cincinnati, she survives the scene of Beloved's murder and becomes the focus of Sethe's life. Sethe thinks of her as "a charmed child" who "pulled the white girl [Amy Denver] out of the hill" to save them both. As the first African-American generation born out of slavery she can make a place for herself in the world in a way that her mother cannot—whether it be a hiding place in the hedge, in her room with her sister, Beloved, at Lady Jones' school, or among the community of women who move to help her and Sethe in their crisis.

Howard (b. 1850) and **Buglar** (b. 1851) are Sethe's sons. They run away from 124 Bluestone Road, the haunting by the baby ghost too terrifying for them to endure.

Paul D Garner is a "Sweet Home man," and a compassionate and empathetic lover who helps Sethe to survive the demands of Beloved and to live with memories of slavery. He has been harnessed like livestock, a bit in his mouth; he sings songs learned on a Georgia chain gang after his attempted escape from Sweet Home; he has known helplessness and humiliation as powerful as Sethe's. Considering his brutal history, he is a remarkably, almost unbelievably, good man.

Halle Suggs is the father of Sethe's children, and the youngest of Baby Suggs' eight children. He works for five years to purchase freedom for his mother who moves to Cincinnati and the house at 124 Bluestone Road. He disappears after the escape from Sweet Home, broken by the sight of Sethe's degradation by the schoolteacher and his nephews.

Baby Suggs (**Grandma Baby**) (1795–1865) is the mother of Halle. In Cincinnati she becomes a spiritual leader in the black community, ministering to men, women, and children, urging them to recognize themselves as loving beings, not brutalized slaves. She dies twenty-eight days after Sethe's arrival with Denver at 124 Bluestone.

Stamp Paid (**Joshua**) is the Kentucky slave who ferries Sethe and Denver across the Ohio River. Earlier, he had delivered her three children to Grandma Baby's house. When Sethe tries to kill her children, he saves Denver.

Amy Denver is the sixteen-year-old, white indentured servant running away to Boston on a quest for "a piece of velvet." She finds Sethe, her feet too swollen to walk, able only to crawl to a nearby shed. Amy massages her feet and soothes Sethe's festering back, likening the forming scars to a chokecherry tree. She helps Sethe in childbirth, then continues her journey, asking that Sethe tell the baby her name.

Mr. Garner is the benign master of Sweet Home. His death leaves the plantation in debt and forces Mrs. Garner to sell their slaves. That he treated his slaves well makes no difference in the fates of the "Sweet Home men" and Sethe, proof that slavery could never be anything but inhumane.

Mrs. Lillian Garner is the wife of Mr. Garner. She is kind to Sethe, but amused when the young girl asks about a ceremony to mark her wedding to Halle. Slaves have no weddings, but she gives Sethe a pair of crystal earrings to mark the occasion. After her husband's death she sells Paul F to settle debts and makes "schoolteacher" overseer.

Schoolteacher is the widowed brother-in-law of Mr. Garner. He foils the escape attempts of the Sweet Home men; observes and coldly records the taking of Sethe's milk by his two nephews; and comes to capture Sethe and her children in Cincinnati. For him, slaves are farm stock and Sethe is valuable as a breeder of new slaves.

Sixo is burned alive by schoolteacher after attempting to escape Sweet Home. As he dies, he sings for his unborn child, "Seven-O! Seven-O!"

Patsy, the Thirty-Mile Woman, carries Sixo's child. She joins the escape from Sweet Home and watches from her hiding place as schoolteacher and his men capture Sixo and Paul D.

Paul A Garner, a Sweet Home man. After he is caught in the escape, tortured, and killed, his "headless, feetless torso" hangs from a tree as proof of his worthlessness.

Paul F Garner, a Sweet Home man, sold by Mrs. Garner to pay plantation debts.

Ma'am is Sethe's mother, a field hand recognizable only by her hat. She reveals to Sethe a tatoo under her breast, a mark by which Sethe may identify her as her mother. When Ma'am is later hanged for some unknown offense, her corpse is too mutilated for Sethe to recognize. On the slave ship from Africa she bears Sethe, the only of her offspring she does not abort or kill, the child of the one man whom she loved.

Nan is the plantation wet-nurse who was brought from Africa on the same slave ship as Ma'am. She tells Sethe the story of her birth and that she is named for her father.

Ella is a conductor on the Underground Railroad who escorts Sethe and the infant Denver to 124 Bluestone Road. A slave herself, she brings food and clothing to Sethe and the infant Denver. She observes, "If anybody was to ask me I'd say, 'Don't love nothing.'"

Lady Jones is the light-skinned teacher who conducts classes in her home for the "unpicked children of Cincinnati." She finds Denver a job, offers her education, and instinctively responds to her emotional need.

Edward Bodwin is a Quaker abolitionist and supporter of the Underground Railroad. His home is a way station, yet he keeps on a shelf a small figurine of a slave on his knees. He secures Sethe's release after her imprisonment. ❀

Critical Views on
Beloved

[In this extract, David Lawrence examines the ghostly
Beloved as a threat to Sethe and the community that must
be exorcised in order to save them both.]

In William Faulkner's *Light in August,* Byron Bunch reflects that no
matter how much a person might "talk about how he'd like to escape
from living folks . . . it's the dead folks that do him the damage." The
damage done by dead folks in Toni Morrison's *Beloved* points to the
central position accorded to memory, the place where these dead
folks are kept alive, in this novel of futile forgetting and persistent
remembrance. Operating independently of the conscious will,
memory is shown to be an active, constitutive force that has the
power to construct and circumscribe identity, both individual and
collective, in the image of its own contents. Sethe's "rememory," in
giving substance to her murdered daughter and to the painful past,
casts its spell over the entire community, drawing the members of
that community into one person's struggle with the torments of a
history that refuses to die.

In portraying the capacity of the past to haunt individual and community life in the present, *Beloved* brings into daylight the "ghosts"
that are harbored by memory and that hold their "hosts" in thrall,
tyrannically dictating thought, emotion, and action. The stories of the
tightly woven network of characters culminate in a ritualistic sacrifice
of Beloved, a ceremony that frees the community from this pervasive
haunting. The supernatural existence of Beloved, who acts as a scapegoat for the evils of the past, threatens the naturalized set of inherited
codes by which the community defines itself. The climactic scene
shows how a culture may find it necessary in a moment of crisis to
exorcise its own demons in order to reaffirm its identity.

Morrison first exposes, however, the workings of the internal mecha-
nisms that have generated the need for exorcism in the first place. A
deeply encoded rejection of the body drives the highly pressurized
haunting in *Beloved.* The black community of Cincinnati is caught

in a cycle of self-denial, a suffocating repression of fundamental bodily needs and wants. The inability to articulate such embodied experience, to find a text for the desiring body within communal codes, obstructs self-knowledge and does violence to the fabric of community. Woven into the dense texture of the novel, into what Morrison has called the "subliminal, the underground life of a novel," the interaction of language and body underlies the collective confrontation with the ghosts of memory. In her representation of this psychic battle, Morrison fashions word and flesh as intimate allies in the project of constructing a domain in which body and spirit may thrive. The exorcism of Beloved, an embodiment of resurgent desire, opens the way to a reworking of the codes that have enforced the silencing of the body's story, making possible a remembering of the cultural heritage that has haunted the characters so destructively. In the end, the communal body seems ready to articulate a reinvigorated language that, in returning to its roots in the body, empowers its speakers to forge a more open, inclusive community.

In a novel that examines the dehumanizing impact of slavery, one might expect that the white man, the monstrous enforcer of slavery's brutality, would haunt the black community. The haunting occurs, however, within a social structure relatively insulated from the white community and, in its most intense form, springs from the "rememory" of an ex-slave in the form of one victimized by slavery. There is nothing mysteriously threatening about whites; on the contrary, "white folks didn't bear speaking on. Everybody knew." Of course, whites "spoke on" their slaves tirelessly, and, in the exploration of political power in the novel, ownership of body and authorship of language are shown to be insidiously linked. Under the regime of white authority, the "blackness" of the slave's body represents for "whitefolks" an animal savagery and moral depravity that, ironically, ends up remaking them in the image of their own fears:

> Whitepeople believed that whatever the manners under every dark skin was a jungle. Swift unnavigable waters, screaming baboons, sleeping snakes, red gums ready for sweet white blood. . . . But it wasn't the jungle blacks brought with them to this place from the other (livable) place. It was the jungle whitefolks planted in them. And it grew. It spread. In, through and after life, it spread, until it invaded the whites who had made it. . . . The screaming baboon lived under their own white skin; the red gums were their own.

This "belief," which underlies the chilling scientific rationality of schoolteacher, abstracts the human corporeality of the slave into a sign for the other in the discourse of the dominant ideology. Further, such invasive signifying upon the black body generates a self-ful-filling prophecy, as blacks find themselves unable to assert an iden-tity outside the expectations imposed upon them: "The more [colored people] used themselves up to persuade whites of some-thing Negroes believed could not be questioned, the deeper and more tangled the jungle grew inside."

In *Beloved,* the question of authority over one's own body is consis-tently related to that of authority over discourse; bodily and linguistic disempowerment frequently intersect. At Sweet Home, Sethe makes the ink with which schoolteacher and his nephews define on paper her "animal characteristics"; the ink, a tool for communication produced by her own hands, is turned against her as ammunition for their "weapons" of torture, pen and paper. Shocked, she asks Mrs. Garner for the definitions of "characteristics" and "features," vainly attempting to assert control over the words that have conscripted her body in a notebook. The terror she feels at seeing herself defined and divided (animal traits on the left, human on the right) concludes her list on ways whites can "dirty you so bad you forgot who you were"; the litany of brutality—decapitations, burnings, rapes—she provides Beloved as "reasons" for killing her ends with this bottom line: "And no one, nobody on this earth, would list her daughter's characteristics on the animal side of the paper. No. Oh no."

—David Lawrence, "Fleshly Ghosts and Ghostly Flesh: The Word and the Body in *Beloved," Studies in American Fiction* 19, no. 2 (Autumn 1991): pp. 189–191.

BERNARD W. BELL ON MORRISON'S WOMANIST REMEMBRANCES OF THINGS PAST

[Bernard W. Bell is Professor of English at Pennsylvania State University. His most recent volume of criticism is *The Afro-American Novel and Its Tradition* (1987). In this extract, Bell discusses *Beloved* as a postmodern romance about the resilience of African Americans.]

On a sociopsychological level, *Beloved* is the story of Sethe Suggs's quest for social freedom and psychological wholeness. Sethe struggles with the haunting memory of her slave past and the retribution of Beloved, the ghost of the infant daughter that she killed in order to save her from the living death of slavery. On a legendary and mythic level, *Beloved* is a ghost story that frames embedded narratives of the impact of slavery, racism, and sexism on the capacity for love, faith, and community of black families, especially of black women, during the Reconstruction period. Set in post-Civil-War Cincinnati, *Beloved* is a womanist neo-slave narrative of double consciousness, a postmodern romance that speaks in many compelling voices and on several time levels of the historical rape of black American women and of the resilient spirit of blacks in surviving as a people. . . .

As the author has explained in the interviews and as a sympathetic white minister's report in the February 12, 1856, issue of the *American Baptist* reveals, at the center of *Beloved* is Morrison's retelling of the chilling historical account of a compassionate yet resolute self-emancipated mother's tough love. Margaret Garner, with the tacit sympathy of her sexagenarian mother-in-law, cut the throat of one of her four children and tried to kill the others to save them from the outrages of slavery that she had suffered. Guided by the spirits of the many thousands gone, as inscribed in her dedication, Morrison employs a multivocal text and a highly figurative language to probe her characters' double consciousness of their terribly paradoxical circumstances as people and non-people in a social arena of white male hegemony. She also foregrounds infanticide as a desperate act of "'thick'" love by a fugitive-slave mother "with iron eyes and backbone to match."

"'Love is or it ain't,'" Sethe, the dramatized narrator/protagonist, says in reproach to a shocked friend, Paul D. "'Thin love ain't love at all.'" Indignantly reflecting on Paul D's metonymic reprimand that she "'got two feet . . . not four,'" she later expands on their oppositional metaphors in reverie: "Too thick, he said. My love was too thick. What he know about it? Who in the world is he willing to die for? Would he give his privates to a stranger in return for a carving?"

The implied author, the version of herself that Morrison creates as she creates the narrative, brilliantly dramatizes the moral, sexual, and epistemological distances between Sethe and Paul D. After their first dialogue, a trackless, quiet forest abruptly appears between them. This metaphorical silence is an ingenious, ironic use of the techniques of call and response that invites the implied reader—in Wolfgang Iser's words, that "network of response-inviting structures, which impel the reader to grasp the text"—to pause and take stock of his or her own ambivalent moral and visceral responses to this slave mother's voicing of her thick love.

Thematically, the implied author interweaves racial and sexual consciousness in *Beloved*. Sethe's black awareness and rejection of white perceptions and inscriptions of herself, her children, and other slaves as non-human—marking them by letter, law, and lash as both animals and property—are synthesized with her black feminist sense of self-sufficiency. Sethe reconciles gender differences with first her husband Halle Suggs, and later Paul D, in heterosexual, endogamous relationships that affirm the natural and Biblical principles of the racial and ethnic survival of peoplehood through procreation and parenting in extended families. Although the implied author blends racial and sexual consciousness, the structure and style of the text foreground the ambivalence of slave women about motherhood that violates their personal integrity and that of their family.

Foregrounding the theme of motherhood, Morrison divides the text into twenty-eight unnumbered mini-sections, the usual number of days in a woman's monthly menstrual cycle, within three larger, disproportionate sections. Within these sections, Sethe experiences twenty-eight happy days of "having women friends, a mother-in-law, and all of her children together; of being part of a neighborhood; of, in fact, having neighbors at all to call her own." Also within these sections, the passion and power of memory ebb and flow in a discontinuous, multivocal discourse of the present with the past. Unlike the univocal, nineteenth-century slave narratives, in which plot rides character in the protagonist's journey of transformation from object to subject, *Beloved* is a haunting story of a mother's love that frames a series of interrelated love stories (maternal, parental, filial, sororal, conjugal, heterosexual, familial, and communal) by multiple narrators. These stories begin in 1873 and end in 1874, but flash back intermittently to 1855. In the flashbacks and reveries, the omniscient narrator invokes ancestral black women's remembrances of the terror and horror of the Middle Passage. She also probes the deep physical and psychic wounds of Southern slavery, especially the paradoxes and perversities of life on Sweet Home plantation in Kentucky, and recalls Sethe's bold flight to freedom in Ohio in 1855. Freedom, as Paul D's and Sethe's stories most dramatically illustrate, is to get to a place where you could love anything you chose—not to need permission for desire.

—Bernard W. Bell, "*Beloved:* A Womanist Neo-Slave Narrative; or Multivocal Remembrances of Things Past," *African American Review* 26, no. 1 (Spring 1992): pp. 8–10.

STEPHANIE A. DEMETRAKOPOULOS ON THE DEATH OF THE MATERNAL IN SETHE

[Stephanie A. Demetrakopoulos teaches at Western Michigan University and has written extensively on the interrelationship of psychology and spirituality in literature. She is co-editor of *New Dimensions of Spirituality: A Biracial and Bicultural Reading of the Novels of Toni Morrison* (1987) and author of *Listening to Our Bodies: The Rebirth of Feminine Wisdom* (1983). In this extract, Demetrakopoulos examines motherhood in *Beloved;* Baby Suggs and Sethe as women defined by maternal bonds and the cruelties of slavery.]

Beloved is, on an historical and sociological level, a Holocaust book, and like much Holocaust literature, it marvels at the indifferent and enduring beauty of nature as a frame for the worst human atrocities. This theme is central to *And the Sun Kept On Shining*, for example, in which the author loses her entire family and then is stripped of her humanity in a Nazi death camp. Similarly, in both Alain Resnais' *Night and Fog* and his recent *Shoah*, the camera lingers ironically on beautiful landscapes as a voice-over comments on the pastoral setting where Jews were slaughtered and buried in mass graves. In Morrison's novel, Sethe marvels at how the beautiful landscape of Sweet Home recurs more often in her memories as a pastoral vision than as the slaughterhouse it finally became. Nature erases atrocities, but this allows humans to repeat them.

The originality of *Beloved* lies in Morrison's delineation of the cruelty of the nature *within*. Her use of the pathetic fallacy ironically underlines the cruel absurdity of maternal passion. After Sethe gives birth to Denver, Morrison comments on the lie of fecundity in their environment. The spores of bluefern floating in the river, she writes,

> are seeds in which the whole generation sleeps confident of a future. And for a moment it is easy to believe that each one has one—will become all of what is contained in the spore: will live out its days as planned. This moment of certainty lasts no longer than that; longer, perhaps than the spore itself.

But tenuous, frail, as almost certainly doomed as newborn life is, the mother instinct takes upon itself total and crushing responsibility for the fruition of its offspring. Sethe repeatedly cites her milk as a kind of panacea, even as the bonding element of her family.

To fully understand the extent to which Sethe's maternal bonds almost destroy her, we must look closely at the life stages that her surviving daughter Denver passes through. Denver's round, brown, chubby body symbolizes the *gravitas* of social reality, of history, which she so prosaically embodies. This is the same prosaic quality suggested by Denver's name, her typically little-girl secret room in the bushes, and her adolescent response to Paul D's entering her mother's life (Denver is both waiting for her father Halle and embarrassed by her mother's sexuality). Like Nel in *Sula* and Hagar in *Song of Solomon*, Denver needs community and family, traditional ties. She is the female survivor in Western culture, the hard-headed practical one who will finally seek work and make connections with the outside world. We see this early in her discovery of Lady Jones's classes; we see her heading for a future in American culture and society at the close of the novel as a young man pursues her down the street; and we have earlier been told that perhaps she will go to Oberlin College. Denver, in short, comes to embody the history that Sethe so resists entering.

In an awesomely strong manner, Denver finally gives birth to her Self, her own Identity. Her mother has ensured Denver's life, her survival; but Sethe has not projected futures for Denver that might ensure the child's ability to step into womanhood. Denver's consciousness as a female emerges for her as she sits alone in her bower (a word that has resonated with sexual connotations since Milton and Spenser's use of bowers as symbols for prelapsarian female sexuality), and her emergent adolescent sexuality is part of what impels her identification with Beloved, who unwittingly provides one step toward maturity for Denver's Womanself, struggling to be born. Part of Denver's strength lies in her genetic heritage: When she goes to look for work, we are told that she is her father's daughter. And Paul D remarks at the conclusion of the novel on how much she looks like Halle, who offers a superb image of male nurturing, industry, and compassion. Coupled with Sethe's strength, the qualities associated with Halle will, we know, carry Denver far.

Denver actually midwives two female souls into the toils of adult individuation—her mother Sethe's as well as her own. Denver helps deliver Sethe from her deadly bond with Beloved. It is from Denver that Sethe takes the word *plans* and by the end of the book is able to apply this concept to herself. Denver uses whatever raw material she finds around her to help her out of the matriarchal cave into life. Even Beloved serves as a foothold, a rung on the ladder; as a woman one step ahead in sexual development. Also, in mothering Beloved, Denver remothers herself away from her fears of Sethe, which began when she accidentally learned of her sister's murder. When Denver tells Sethe's story to Beloved, she really *knows* it for the first time; it becomes far more than just words, the myth of her own origin. She begins to understand how her mother suffered and finally becomes protective of Sethe as she sees the actual flesh of Sethe disappearing in the devouring bond with Beloved. Denver is realistic enough to see that something must be done, and it is through her agency that the community of women mobilize to exorcise Beloved. Sethe is tied only to her past, whereas Denver is interested only in the present until she matures to become the caretaker of her caretaker and enters the future. For a time, Denver must precociously become Demeter, until Paul D returns to catalyze Sethe out of her sickbed. The live daughter as rescuer supplants the dead daughter as succubus. Sethe's girl child does finally mean her life.

—Stephanie A. Demetrakopoulos, "Maternal Bonds as Devourers of Women's Individuation in Toni Morrison's *Beloved*," *African American Review* 26, no. 1 (Spring 1992): pp. 54–56.

[Linda Krumholz has recently taught American literature as
a Visiting Assistant Professor at Oberlin College. In this
extract, Krumholz discusses *Beloved* as Morrison's recon-
ceptualization of American history.]

Morrison uses ritual as a model for the healing process. Rituals function as formal events in which symbolic representations—such as
dance, song, story, and other activities—are spiritually and communally endowed with the power to shape real relations in the world. In
Beloved, ritual processes also imply particular notions of pedagogy
and epistemology in which—by way of contrast with dominant
Western traditions—knowledge is multiple, context-dependent, col-
lectively asserted, and spiritually derived. Through her assertion of
the transformative power of ritual and the incorporation of rituals
of healing into her narrative, Morrison invests the novel with the
potential to construct and transform individual consciousness as
well as social relations.

To make the novel work as a ritual, Morrison adapts techniques
from Modernist novels, such as the fragmentation of the plot and a
shifting narrative voice, to compel the reader to actively construct an
interpretive framework. In *Beloved* the reader's process of recon-
structing the fragmented story parallels Sethe's psychological
recovery: Repressed fragments of the (fictionalized) personal and
historical past are retrieved and reconstructed. Morrison also introduces oral narrative techniques—repetition, the blending of voices, a
shifting narrative voice, and an episodic framework—that help to
simulate the aural, participatory dynamics of ritual within the private, introspective form of the novel. In many oral traditions, storytelling and poetry are inseparable from ritual, since words as sounds
are perceived as more than concepts; they are events with consequences. Morrison uses Modernist and oral techniques in conjunc-
tion with specifically African-American cultural referents, both
historical and symbolic, to create a distinctly African-American
voice and vision which, as in Baby Suggs's rituals, invoke the spiritual and imaginative power to teach and to heal.

The central ritual of healing—Sethe's "rememory" of and confrontation with her past—and the reader's ritual of healing correspond to the

three sections of the novel. In part one the arrival first of Paul D then of Beloved forces Sethe to confront her past in her incompatible roles as a slave and as a mother. Moving from the fall of 1873 to the winter, the second part describes Sethe's period of atonement, during which she is enveloped by the past, isolated in her house with Beloved, who forces her to suffer over and over again all the pain and shame of the past. Finally, part three is Sethe's ritual "cleaning," in which the women of the community aid her in casting out the voracious Beloved, and Sethe experiences a repetition of her scene of trauma with a difference—this time she aims her murderous hand at the white man who threatens her child.

The three phases of the reader's ritual also involve a personal reckoning with the history of slavery. In part one, stories of slavery are accumulated through fragmented recollections, culminating in the revelation of Sethe's murder of her child in the last chapters of the section. In part two, the reader is immersed in the voices of despair. Morrison presents the internal voices of Sethe, Denver, and Beloved in a ritual chant of possession, while Paul D and Stamp Paid are also overwhelmed by the legacy of slavery. The last part of the novel is the reader's "clearing," achieved through the comic relief of the conversation of Paul D and Stamp Paid and the hopeful reunion of Sethe and Paul D. The novel concludes with Denver's emergence as the new teacher, providing the reader with a model for a new pedagogy and the opportunity for the reconstruction of slave history from a black woman's perspective.

Finally, while *Beloved* can be read as a ritual of healing, there is also an element of disruption and unease in the novel, embodied in the character of Beloved. As an eruption of the past and the repressed unconscious, Beloved catalyzes the healing process for the characters and for the reader; thus, she is a disruption necessary for healing. But Beloved also acts as a trickster figure who defies narrative closure or categorization, foreclosing the possibility of a complete "clearing" for the reader. Thus, as the reader leaves the book, we have taken on slavery's haunt as our own.

—Linda Krumholz, "The Ghosts of Slavery: Historical Recovery in Toni Morrison's *Beloved*," *African American Review* 26, no. 3 (Fall 1992): pp. 396–397.

ASHRAF H. D. RUSHDY ON SETHE'S PROCESS OF HEALING

[Ashraf H. D. Rushdy is author of *The Empty Garden: The Subject of Late Milton* (1992). In this extract, Rushdy proposes that Sethe's infanticide is impossible to judge apart from the circumstances of slavery.]

The obvious place to begin a reading tracing Morrison's signifyin(g) on the story of Margaret Garner is the site of infanticide. One of the recurrent tropes of the African American novel of slavery is the possible response to an institution attempting to render meaningless the mother-child relationship. In William Wells Brown's *Clotelle*, the slave mother Isabella would rather commit suicide than face slavery for herself and her children. Hunted by a crowd of dogs and slave-catchers, Isabella leaps into the Potomac as an act symbolizing the "unconquerable love of liberty which the human heart may inherit." The chapter is entitled "Death Is Freedom." In Zora Neale Hurston's *Moses, Man of the Mountain*, slavery is described as an institution in which only death can give freedom. As Amram tells Caleb, "you are up against a hard game when you got to die to beat it." It is an even harder game, Morrison would add, when you have to kill what you love most.

Coffin explicitly states Margaret's motivation: "the slave mother . . . killed her child rather than see it taken back to slavery." Like Harriet Jacobs, Margaret, in Coffin's reading of her history, sees death as a better alternative than slavery. "It seemed to me," writes Jacobs, "that I would rather see them [her children] killed than have them given up to his [the slaveowner's] power . . . When I lay down beside my child, I felt how much easier it would be to see her die than to see her master beat her about."

Sethe killed Beloved, according to Stamp Paid, because she "was trying to outhurt the hurters." "She love those children." Loving as a slave, according to Paul D (whom Stamp Paid is trying to persuade with his assessment of Sethe's motivation), meant loving small, loving in an unobvious way so that whatever was loved did not become part of a technique of punishment. Paul D's advice, and his credo, was to "love just a little bit" so that when the slave owners took whatever or whoever the slave loved and "broke its back, or shoved it in a croaker sack, well, maybe you'd have a little love left over for the next one." Ella, another ex-slave who was loved by no one and who considered "love a serious disability," lived by the simple dictum "Don't love nothing." When Paul D learns of Sethe's infanticide he tells her that her love is "too thick." She responds by telling him that "Love is or it ain't. Thin love ain't love at all." Although Paul D lives by his philosophy of loving small as a protective measure, he knows what Sethe means. "He knew exactly what she meant: to get to a place where you could love anything you chose—not to need permission for desire—well now, *that* was freedom." Although Paul D knows the conditions of freedom and Sethe knows the conditions of love, each has to learn to claim that freedom, to claim that love, and thereby to claim genuine community and begin the process of healing.

Sethe's process of healing occurs when she acknowledges her act and accepts her responsibility for it while also recognizing the reason for her act within a framework larger than that of individual resolve. Here, perhaps, is Morrison's most powerful introjection into the Margaret Garner story—the establishing of a context for Sethe's act. Sethe's own mother kills all the children fathered by the whites who raped her. As Nan, Sethe's grandmother tells her, "She threw them all away but you. The one from the crew she threw away on the island. The others from more whites she also threw away. Without names, she threw them." Another important person helping Sethe through the exorcising of her painful memories is Ella, who, it is hinted, has also committed infanticide. By placing such a frame around Sethe's story, Morrison insists on the impossibility of judging an action without reference to the terms of its enactment—the wrongness of assuming a transhistorical ethic outside a particular historical moment. Morrison is not justifying Sethe's actions; she is writing about them in the only way she knows how—through eyes that accuse and embrace, through a perspective that criticizes while it rejoices. Towards that end, she has constructed two daughterly presences in her novel who help Sethe remember and forget her personal history, who embody the dual perspective of critique and rejoicing.

Beloved, the incarnation of the ghost of the murdered daughter, is the most obvious revisionist construction in Morrison's novel. Through Beloved, she signifies on history by resurrecting one of its anonymous victims. When Beloved comes back to haunt Sethe for murdering her, Beloved becomes the incarnated memory of Sethe's guilt. Moreover, she is nothing but guilt, a symbol of an unrelenting criticism of the dehumanizing function of the institution of slavery. In this, she is the daughter representing a severe critique, demonstrating the determinism in slave history. She represents, however, only half of Morrison's work: the accusing glare, the unforgiving perspective, the need to forget—"It was not a story to pass on." There is another daughter in the novel, another daughter of history—representing the embracing glance, the loving view, the need to remember.

When Sethe first sees the reincarnated Beloved, her "bladder filled to capacity." She runs immediately to the outhouse, but does not make it: "Right in front of its door she had to lift her skirts, and the water she voided was endless. Like a horse, she thought, but as it went on and on she thought, No, more like flooding the boat when Denver was born. So much water Amy said, 'Hold on, Lu. You going to sink us you keep that up.' But there was no stopping water breaking from a breaking womb and there was no stopping now." She would later, in a retrospective moment, remember this scene in trying to discover who Beloved could be. What is worth noticing, though, is that at that precise moment she does not remember the birth of Beloved but the birth of Denver. Denver is the fictional recreation of Margaret Garner's other daughter, the daughter who survives. Coffin describes Garner and this daughter in the courtroom: "The babe she held in her arms was a little girl, about nine months old, and was much lighter in color than herself, light enough to show a red tinge in its cheek." In *Beloved,* Denver becomes the daughter of hope.

—Ashraf H. D. Rushdy "Daughters Signifyin(g) History: The Example of Toni Morrison's *Beloved,*" *American Literature* 64, no. 3 (September 1992): pp. 576–578.

[In this extract, Caroline Rody notes how Denver, the inheritor of the story, will take Sethe's family exodus saga into the larger American culture.]

In the "village" of *Beloved,* the multigenerational, culture-bearing black community of Morrison's ideal appears in devastated form, in the persons of a few traumatized survivors, eking out an existence in the aftermath of slavery. Foregrounded in the novel, the telling of stories becomes memory's struggle with catastrophe and loss. For Morrison's characters, as for the novel in its contemporary moment, cultural transmission requires the retrieval of traumatic memories. This "history" thus acquires the function of communal "talking cure": its characters, author, and readers delve into the past, repeating painful stories to work toward the health of fuller awareness.

Beloved opens upon the haunted house where, shunned by the neighborhood, Morrison's heroine Sethe is raising her daughter Denver in an atmosphere of stagnant grief. Together they have come to accept what drove two sons away from home: the "spiteful" baby ghost who makes hand prints in the cake. Into this scene walks Paul D, that rare "kind of man who could walk into a house and make the women cry." His arrival changes the climate of repression: he chases the invisible haunter from the house and sparks in Sethe "the temptation to trust and remember," "to go ahead and feel," for the first time in years. His past, too, has required profound repression: he has a "tobacco tin buried in his chest where a red heart used to be. Its lid rusted shut." Together, Sethe and Paul D begin a mutual talking cure that promises a mutual future. As their halting, gradual storytelling is taken up by other characters, the novel's present unfolds entwined in multiple strands of time, voice, incident, and perspective.

Storytelling becomes the text's self-conscious task; many scenes present a character narrating his or her life to a listener. The novel's distinctive tone arises from the very difficulty of telling for those recovering from the traumas of slavery—witnessing the murder, torture, or sale of family and friends; being whipped, chained, led with an iron bit in the mouth, and housed in an underground "box"; being examined and catalogued in terms of "human" and "animal" characteristics, or forcibly "nursed" by white boys when one's breasts held milk for a baby. These experiences fragment and block the memories of Morrison's ex-slaves, whose stories are revealed in bits, out of sequence, in a painful eking out and holding back often rendered in spare synecdoche: "Paul D had only begun . . . when her fingers on his knee, soft and reassuring, stopped him. . . . Saying more might push them both to a place they couldn't get back from. Sethe rubbed and rubbed. . . . She hoped it calmed him as it did her. Like kneading bread . . . working dough. Nothing better than that to start the day's serious work of beating back the past."

As the narrative loops around events, dramatizing pain's effect on memory, it also suggests a hesitance to force the past out of characters whose memories stand in for the suffering of innumerable unknown people. Any recuperations are performed against a blank background of storylessness, symbolic of our historical knowledge of African Americans and of their representation in our literature. Morrison chooses just one family's haunted house to explicate, but as Grandma Baby Suggs says, "Not a house in the country ain't packed to the rafters with some dead Negro's grief." Every American house is a haunted house. As *Beloved* revives the past in the modes of haunting, memory, and storytelling, it becomes an exercise in the poetics of absence.

Morrison's prose inventively represents the multiple shades of loss and absence known to slaves: "Anybody Baby Suggs knew, let alone loved, who hadn't run off or been hanged, got rented out, loaned out, bought up, brought back, stored up, mortgaged, won, stolen, or seized." Characters tend to gather around them clusters of the lost. "Did Patty lose her lisp?" Baby Suggs wonders about the children sold from her; "what color did Famous' skin finally take?" On his postwar trek north, Paul D saw "twelve dead blacks in the first eighteen miles," and "by the time he got to Mobile, he had seen more dead people than living ones." A traveling man, Paul D brings to the text a voice of tribal griot-cum-historical eyewitness: "During, before, and after the war he had seen Negroes so stunned, or hungry, or tired or bereft it was a wonder they recalled or said anything. Who, like him, had hidden in caves and fought owls for food . . . stole from pigs . . . slept in trees in the day and walked by night. . . . Once he met a Negro about fourteen years old who lived by himself in the woods and said he couldn't remember living anywhere else. He saw a witless colored woman jailed and hanged for stealing ducks she believed were her own babies. Pas-

sages like this bring to the novel cinematic visions of an entire struggling people, among whom Morrison names a precious few characters for detailed narration. The reader learns, like Ella as she aids
escaping slaves, to listen "for the holes—the things the fugitives did
not say, the questions they did not ask . . . the unnamed, unmen-
tioned people left behind." To demarcate the "holes" Morrison has
characters repeat isolated remembered details, metonymies for unre-
countable emotional experiences, the more poignant for their
banality. Baby Suggs recalls, "My first-born. All I can remember of
her is how she loved the burned bottom of bread. Can you beat that?
Eight children and that's all I remember."

—Caroline Rody, "Toni Morrison's *Beloved*: History, 'Rememory,' and
a 'Clamor for a Kiss,'" *American Literary History* 7, no. 1 (Spring
1995): pp. 99–101.

PAMELA E. BARNETT ON IMAGES OF RAPE AND THE SUPERNATURAL IN *BELOVED*

[Pamela E. Barnett is visiting assistant professor of English at
Emory University. Her articles have appeared in *Women's
Studies and Signs;* the essay published in this volume is part
of her current, book-length project, *The Language of Rape:
Sexual Violence and Late-Twentieth-Century American Nar-
rative.* In this extract, Barnett examines the ways in which
Sethe's memories of sexual abuse hold particular power.]

Toni Morrison's *Beloved* is haunted by history, memory, and a
specter that embodies both; yet it would be accurate to say that
Beloved is haunted by the history and memory of rape specifically.
While Morrison depicts myriad abuses of slavery like brutal beatings
and lynchings, the depictions of and allusions to rape are of primary
importance; each in some way helps explain the infanticide that
marks the beginnings of Sethe's story as a free woman. Sethe kills
her child so that no white man will ever "dirty" her, so that no young
man with "mossy teeth" will ever hold the child down and suck her
breasts. Of all the memories that haunt Morrison's characters, those

that involve sexual abuse and exploitation hold particular power: rape is the trauma that forces Paul D to lock his many painful memories in a "tobacco tin" heart, that Sethe remembers more vividly than the beating that leaves a tree of scars on her back, that destroys Halle's mind, and against which Ella measures all evil.

I say that the book is haunted by rape not to pun idly on the ghostly presence that names the book but to establish the link between haunting and rape that invigorates the novel's dominant trope: the succubus figure. The character Beloved is not just the ghost of Sethe's dead child; she is a succubus, a female demon and nightmare figure that sexually assaults male sleepers and drains them of semen. The succubus figure, which is related to the vampire, another sexualized figure that drains vital fluid, was incorporated into African American folklore in the form of shapeshifting witches who "ride" terrified victims in the night, and Beloved embodies the qualities of that figure as well. In separate assaults, Beloved drains Paul D of semen and Sethe of vitality; symptomatically, Beloved's body swells as she also feeds off her victims' horrible memories of and recurring nightmares about sexual violations that occurred in their enslaved past. But Beloved functions as more than the receptacle of remembered stories; she reenacts sexual violation and thus figures the persistent nightmares common to survivors of trauma. Her insistent manifestation constitutes a challenge for the characters who have survived rapes inflicted while they were enslaved: directly, and finally communally, to confront a past they cannot forget. Indeed, it is apparent forgetting that subjects them to traumatic return; confrontation requires a direct attempt at remembering.

Morrison uses the succubus figure to represent the effects of institutionalized rape under slavery. When the enslaved persons' bodies were violated, their reproductive potential was commodified. The succubus, who rapes and steals semen, is metaphorically linked to such rapes and to the exploitation of African Americans' reproduction. Just as rape was used to dehumanize enslaved persons, the succubus or vampire's assault robs victims of vitality, both physical and psychological. By representing a female rapist figure and a male rape victim, Morrison foregrounds race, rather than gender, as the category determining domination or subjection to rape.

Two memories of rape that figure prominently in the novel echo the succubus's particular form of sexual assault. The narrator refers several times to the incident in which two "mossy-toothed" boys hold Sethe down and suck her breast milk. No less important, Paul D works on a chain gang in Alfred, Georgia, where prisoners are forced to fellate white guards every morning. In addition, Ella is locked up and repeatedly raped by a father and son she calls "the lowest yet," and Stamp Paid's wife, Vashti, is forced into sex by her enslaver. Baby Suggs is compelled to have sex with a straw boss who later breaks his coercive promise not to sell her child and again with an overseer. Sethe's mother is "taken up many times by the crew" during the Middle Passage, as are many other enslaved women. And three women in the novel—Sethe's mother, Baby Suggs, and Ella— refuse to nurse babies conceived through rape. Other allusions to sexual violation include the Sweet Home men's dreams of rape, Sethe's explanation for adopting the mysterious Beloved—her fears that white men will "jump on" a homeless, wandering black girl— and the neighborhood suspicion that Beloved is the black girl rumored to have been imprisoned and sexually enslaved by a local white man who has recently died. There are also acts of desperate prostitution that are akin to rape: Sethe's exchange of sex for the engraving on her baby's tombstone and the Saturday girls' work at the slaughterhouse.

These incidents of rape frame Sethe's explanation for killing her baby daughter. Sethe tries to tell the furious Beloved that death actually protected the baby from the deep despair that killed Baby Suggs, from "what Ella knew, what Stamp saw and what made Paul D tremble": horrific experiences and memories of rape. Whites do "not just work, kill, or maim you, but dirty you," Sethe tells Beloved, "Dirty you so bad you [can't] like yourself anymore." Sethe passionately insists that she protected her beloved daughter and also herself from "undreamable dreams" in which "a gang of whites invaded her daughter's private parts, soiled her daughter's thighs and threw her daughter out of the wagon." For Sethe, being brutally over-worked, maimed, or killed is subordinate to the overarching horror of being raped and "dirtied" by whites; even dying at the hands of one's mother is subordinate to rape.

—Pamela E. Barnett, "Figurations of Rape and the Supernatural in *Beloved*," *PMLA* 112, no. 3 (May 1997): pp. 418–419.

Works by
Toni Morrison

The Bluest Eye. 1970.

Sula. 1973.

Song of Solomon. 1977.

Tar Baby. 1981.

Dreaming Emmett (play). 1986.

Beloved. 1987.

Jazz. 1992.

Playing in the Dark: Whiteness and the Literary Imagination. 1992.

Birth of a Nation'hood: Gaze, Script, and Spectacle in the O.J. Simpson Case (co-editor with Claudia Brodsky Lacour). 1997.

Paradise. 1998.

Works about
Toni Morrison

Atwood, Margaret. "Haunted by Their Neighbors," *The New York Times Book Review* (September 13, 1987): 49–50.

Awkward, Michael. *Inspiriting Influences: Tradition, Revision, and Afro-American Women's Novels.* New York: Columbia University Press, 1989. 81–88.

Benston, Kimberly W. "Re-weaving the 'Ulysses Scene': Enchantment, Post-Oedipal Identity, and the Buried Text of Blackness in Toni Morrison's *Song of Solomon*," *Comparative American Identities: Race, Sex, and Nationality in the Modern Text.* Ed. Hortense J. Spillers. New York: Routledge, 1991.

Blake, Susan L. "Folklore and Community in Song of Solomon," *MELUS* 7 (1980): 77–82.

Bloom Harold, ed. *Toni Morrison's Beloved.* Philadelphia: Chelsea House, 1999.

———. *Toni Morrison's Song of Solomon.* Philadelphia: Chelsea House, 1999.

———. *Toni Morrison's Sula.* Philadelphia: Chelsea House, 1999.

———. *Toni Morrison's The Bluest Eye.* Philadelphia: Chelsea House, 1999.

Bowers, Susan. "*Beloved* and the New Apocalypse," *The Journal of Ethnic Studies* 18:1 (Spring 1990): 59–75.

Christian, Barbara. "Community and Nature: The Novels of Toni Morrison," *Journal of Ethnic Studies* 7 (February 1980): 65–78.

Clark, Norris. "Flying Back: Toni Morrison's *The Bluest Eye, Sula, and Song of Solomon*," *Minority Voices* 4 (Fall 1980): 51–63.

Cowart, David. "Faulkner and Joyce in Morrison's *Song of Solomon*," *American Literature* 62 (March 1990): 87–100.

Crouch, Stanley. "Aunt Medea," *New Republic* (October 19, 1987): 38–43.

Davis, Cynthia. "Self, Society and Myth in Toni Morrison's Fiction," *Contemporary Literature* 23:3 (1982): 323–342.

De Arman, Charles. "Milkman as the Archetypal Hero: 'Thursday's Child has Far to Go,'" *Obsidian* 6 (Winter 1980): 56–59.

Dickerson, Vanessa D. "The Naked Father in Toni Morrison's *The Bluest Eye*," *Refiguring the Father: New Feminist Readings of Patriarchy*. Eds., Patricia Yaeger and Beth Kowaleski-Wallace. Carbondale: University of Illinois Press, 1989. 108–127.

Flick, Thomas H. "Toni Morrison's 'Allegory of the Cave': Movies, Consumption, and Platonic Realism in *The Bluest Eye*," *The Journal of the Midwest Modern Language Association* (Spring 1989): 110–122.

Harris, Leslie A. "Myth as Structure in Toni Morrison's *Song of Solomon*," *MELUS* 7:3 (Fall 1980): 71.

Harris, Trudier. "Reconnecting Fragments: Afro-American Folk Tradition in *The Bluest Eye*," *Critical Essays on Toni Morrison*. Ed., Nellie Y. McKay. Boston: G. K. Hall, 1988. 68–76.

Horvitz, Deborah. "Nameless Ghosts: Possession and Dispossession in *Beloved*," *Studies in American Fiction* 17 (1989): 157–167.

Hovet, Grace Ann, and Barbara Lounsberry. "Flying as Symbol and Legend in Toni Morrison's *The Bluest Eye, Sula,* and *Song of Solomon*," *CLA Journal* 27:2 (December 1983): 119–140.

Keenan, Sally. " 'Four Hundred Years of Silence': Myth, History, and Motherhood in Toni Morrison's *Beloved*," *Recasting the World: Writing after Colonialism*. Jonathan White, ed. Baltimore: Johns Hopkins University Press, 1993. 45–81.

Klottman, Phyllis R. "Dick-and-Jane and the Shirley Temple Sensibility in *The Bluest Eye*," *Black American Literature Forum* 13 (September 1979): 123–125.

Kubitschek, Missy Dehn. *Claiming the Heritage: African-American Women Novelists and History*. Jackson: University Press of Mississippi, 1991. 174, 177.

Lee, Dorothy H. "*Song of Solomon:* To Ride the Air," *Black American Literature Forum* 16:2 (Summer 1982): 64–70.

Marshall, Brenda. "The Gospel According to Pilate," *American Literature* 57 (October 1985): 486–549.

Mobley, Marilyn Sanders. "A Different Remembering: Memory, History and Meaning in Toni Morrison's *Beloved*," *Modern Critical Views: Toni Morrison*, edited by Harold Bloom. New York: Chelsea House,1988.

Ogunyemi, Chikwenye O. "Order and Disorder in Toni Morrison's *The Bluest Eye*," *Critique* 19:1 (1977): 112–120.

Otten, Terry. *The Crime of Innocence in the Fiction of Toni Morrison*. Columbia: University of Missouri Press, 1989. 82–83.

Page, Philip. "Circularity in Toni Morrison's *Beloved*," *African American Review* 26:1 (Spring 1992): 31–40.

Pinsker, Sanford. "Magic, Realism, Historical Truth, and the Quest for a Liberating Identity: Reflections on Alex Haley's *Roots* and Toni Morrison's *Song of Solomon*," *Studies in Black American Literature Vol. I: Black American Prose Theory*, eds. Joe Weixlmann and Chester J. Fontenot. Greenwood, FL: Penkevill Press, 1984. 183–197.

Portales, Marco. "Toni Morrison's *The Bluest Eye:* Shirley Temple and Cholly," *The Centennial Review* 30 (Fall 1986): 496–506.

Rosenberg, Ruth. " 'And the Children May Know Their Names': Toni Morrison's *Song of Solomon*," *Literary Onomastic Studies* 8 (1981): 195–219.

———. "Seeds in Hard Ground: Black Girlhood in *The Bluest Eye*," *Black American Literature Forum* 21 (Winter 1987): 435–445.

Royster, Philip M. "Milkman's Flying: The Scapegoat Transcended in Toni Morrison's *Song of Solomon*," *CLA Journal* 24 (June 1981): 419–440.

Sale, Maggie. "Call and Response as Critical Method: African-American Oral Traditions and *Beloved*," *African American Review* 26:1 (Spring 1992): 41–50.

Sale, Roger. "Toni Morrison's *Beloved*" (originally "American Novels, 1988"), *Massachusetts Review* 29:1 (Spring 1988): 81–86.

Samuels, Wilfred D., and Clenora Hudson-Weems. " 'Ripping the Veil': Meaning through Rememory in *Beloved*," *Toni Morrison*. Boston: Twayne, 1990. 94–138.

Sargent, Robert. "A Way of Ordering Experience: A Study of Toni Morrison's *The Bluest Eye* and *Sula*," *Faith of a (Woman) Writer*, eds. Alice Kessler-Harris and William McBrien. Westport, CT: Greenwood Press, 1988. 229–236.

Sitter, Deborah Ayer. "The Making of a Man: Dialogic Meaning in *Beloved*," *African American Review* 26:1 (Spring 1992): 17–30.

Smith, Valerie. "The Quest for and Discovery of Identity in Toni Morrison's *Song of Solomon*," *Southern Review* 21 (Summer 1985): 721–732.

————. " 'Circling the Subject': History and Narrative in *Beloved*," *Toni Morrison: Critical Perspectives Past and Present*. K.A. Appiah and Henry Louis Gates Jr., eds. New York: Amistad, 1993. 340–54.

Spallino, Chiara. "*Song of Solomon*: an Adventure in Structure," *Callaloo* 8 (Fall 1985): 510–24.

Tignor, Eleanor Q. "Toni Morrison's Pecola: A Portrait in Pathos," *MAWA Review* 1 (Spring 1982): 24–27.

Valade, Roger M. III, "Post Aesthetic Movement," *The Essential Black Literature Guide*. New York: Visible Ink Press, 1996.

Weever, Jacqueline de. "The Inverted World of Toni Morrison's *The Bluest Eye* and *Sula*," *CLA Journal* 22:4 (June 1979): 402–414.

————. "Toni Morrison's Use of Fairy Tale, Folk Tale and Myth in *Song of Solomon*," *Southern Folklore Quarterly* 44 (1980): 131–144.

Wegs, Joyce M. "Toni Morrison's *Song of Solomon*: A Blues Song," *Essays in Literature* 9:2 (Fall 1982): 211–223.

Index of
Themes and Ideas

MORRISON, TONI, 8; biography of, 10–12

PARADISE, 11

SONG OF SOLOMON, 11, 56–81; Guitar Bains in, 57, 58, 59–60, 61, 63, 64, 65–66, 67, 68, 69, 75; Mrs. Bains in, 57; Boy-Boy in, 65; Susan Byrd in, 73, 74; characters in, 62–63; complexity in male characters in, 64–66; Reverend Cooper in, 60, 80; critical views on, 9, 21, 31, 64–81; First Corinthians (Corrie) Dead in, 56, 59, 60, 62, 64, 67, 69; Hagar Dead in, 57, 58, 59, 61, 63, 67–69, 72, 73, 74, 75, 77, 78, 98; Lena Dead in, 56, 59, 62, 67, 78; Macon Dead in, 56–57, 58, 59, 60, 61, 64, 66, 70, 80; Macon Dead, Sr. in, 59, 60, 65, 80; Milkman Dead in, 9, 57–60, 61, 62, 64, 65–66, 67–68, 69–81; Milkman Dead's heroic quest in, 79–81; Milkman Dead's race and class consciousness in, 76–79; Pilate Dead in, 56, 57, 59, 60, 61, 63, 65, 66, 67, 68, 69, 71, 72, 74, 78, 79, 81; Reba Dead in, 57, 58, 61, 63, 67, 68; Ruth Foster Dead in, 56, 57–58, 60, 61, 62, 69–72, 77–78; Freddie in, 56, 57, 79; Fred Garnett in, 80; ironies of male epic in, 72–76; male flight in, 72–76; mother/son conflict in, 69–72; needs of Hagar's feminine typology in, 67–69; plot summary of, 56–61; Henry Porter in, 60, 64–65, 69; Robert Smith in, 56, 59; Sweet in, 73, 74, 77

SULA, 11, 32–55; Ajax (Albert Jackson) in, 35, 38, 47, 68; binary oppositions in, 39–42; Cecile in, 32–33; characters in, 37–38; Chicken Little in, 33–34, 36, 40, 41, 51, 52; community's use of Sula's evil nature in, 45–47; critical views on, 21, 39–55, 64, 75, 76; deweys in, 40, 41; folklore in, 53–55; Jude Greene in, 34, 35, 38, 43, 44, 47, 52; Nel Wright Greene in, 32, 33, 34, 35, 36, 37, 41–42, 43, 47, 49, 50, 51, 52, 53, 65, 98; land and identity in, 49–52; mythical community in, 42–44; Eva Peace in, 32, 33, 34, 35, 36, 37, 40, 47, 51, 52, 53, 54; Hanna Peace in, 34, 37, 41, 47, 52, 54; Plum (Ralph) Peace in, 33, 34, 38, 40; Sula Peace in, 31, 32, 33–35, 36, 37, 39, 41–42, 43, 44, 45–49, 50, 51, 52, 53, 54, 65, 67, 68, 69, 78; plot summary of, 32–36; Rochelle in, 33; as satire, 39–42; Shadrock in, 32, 34, 35, 37, 42, 46, 47, 51, 52, 53, 54, 64; shifting patterns of accountability in, 49–52; Tar Baby in, 40; Helene Sabat Wright in, 32–33, 38, 41; Wiley Wright in, 33

TAR BABY, 11, 21